When the Eagle Screamed: The Romantic

Horizon in American Diplomacy, 1800–1860

AMERICA IN CRISIS

A series of eight books on American Diplomatic History

EDITOR: *Robert A. Divine*

When the Eagle Screamed

The Romantic Horizon in American Diplomacy

1800–1860

WILLIAM H. GOETZMANN

University of Texas

John Wiley & Sons, Inc.   New York • London • Sydney

Library of Congress Catalog Card Number: 66-26743
PRINTED IN THE UNITED STATES OF AMERICA.

Foreword

"THE UNITED STATES always wins the war and loses the peace," runs a persistent popular complaint. Neither part of the statement is accurate. The United States barely escaped the War of 1812 with its territory intact, and in Korea in the 1950's the nation was forced to settle for a stalemate on the battlefield. At Paris in 1782, and again in 1898, American negotiators drove hard bargains to win notable diplomatic victories. Yet the myth persists, along with the equally erroneous American belief that we are a peaceful people. Our history is studded with conflict and violence. From the Revolution to the Cold War, Americans have been willing to fight for their interests, their beliefs, and their ambitions. The United States has gone to war for many objectives —for independence in 1775, for honor and trade in 1812, for territory in 1846, for humanity and empire in 1898, for neutral rights in 1917, and for national security in 1941. Since 1945 the nation has been engaged in a deadly struggle to contain communism and defend the democratic way of life.

The purpose of this series is to examine in detail eight critical periods relating to American involvement in foreign war from the Revolution through the Cold War. Each author has set out to recount anew the breakdown of diplomacy that led to war and the subsequent quest for peace. The emphasis is on foreign policy, and no effort is made to chronicle the military participation of the United States in these wars. Instead the authors focus on the day-by-day conduct of diplomacy to explain why the nation went to war and to show how peace was restored. Each volume is a synthesis combining the research of other historians with new insights to provide a fresh interpretation of a critical period in

American diplomatic history. It is hoped that this series will help dispel the illusion of national innocence and give Americans a better appreciation of their country's role in war and peace.

ROBERT A. DIVINE

Preface and Acknowledgments

MOST OF THE FACTS upon which this book is based are already well known and can be checked in the standard works on the particular subjects dealt with here. Therefore, since my primary purpose is one of interpretation, I have adhered to the general format of this series and have omitted footnote citations dealing with well-known facts or events. However, I have provided documentation for significant quotations, little-known facts, and points about which there might be some doubt in the minds of readers. Generally, the authorities that I have used can be found in "Suggestions for Further Reading" at the end of the book. In addition, I have drawn heavily upon materials from my two previous, more ambitious works dealing with the period.* And I have drawn upon my years of teaching in a seminar on "Romanticism in America" at Yale University. I am grateful to the members of this seminar for this experience.

I also wish to thank Professor Robert A. Divine and William L. Gum for their patience, Mrs. Michele Aldrich for her assistance in compiling and checking the bibliography, and the secretaries in the History and American Studies Departments of the University of Texas for telling solicitous students that I was away on "vacation." Most of all, I wish to thank my wife, Mewes, and my children, Will, Anne, and Stephen, who suffered neglect so that I might embark on this historical adventure.

Austin, Texas   W. H. GOETZMANN
August 1965

* *Army Exploration in the American West, 1803-1863* (New Haven: Yale University Press, 1959), and *Exploration and Empire* (New York: Alfred A. Knopf, 1966).

Contents

MAPS

(Maps by John V. Morris)

Introduction

IN GENERAL, this book has a single intellectual purpose. It is to place mid-nineteenth-century American expansion in its proper context—that of a worldwide confrontation with exotic lands, alien peoples, and foreign governments which marked the self-conscious emergence of America on the romantic horizon of global diplomacy. In the period between 1800 and 1860 venturesome Americans, imbued with a sense of mission and destiny, ranged all over the globe establishing contact with the known and the unknown, the hostile and the friendly, from Van Diemen's Land to the Arctic Circle. By the end of the period they had· not only secured and settled the vast western interior of North America, they had made a global commitment that was virtually irrevocable. In effect what they had done was to establish a series of borders or frontiers around the world where the United States was brought into direct and often precarious competition with the great powers of the globe. Once these frontiers were established, disengagement was impossible, and it can be argued that the far-flung imperialism that came with the Spanish-American War, the subsequent involvement in Asia, the Latin American entanglements, the crusades in Europe, and all of our precarious Cold War commitments are merely consequences or logical extensions of positions taken long ago in the age of Manifest Destiny.

It has become a fashionable cliché among American historians to refer to the mid-nineteenth century as the "Age of Free Security," meaning that, protected by the great oceans, the British navy, and the absence of formal European alliances, Americans were left free to turn their attention to the interior—to grow and develop and expand across the great empty continent.[1] Citing statistics on the size of our miniature army and our lilliputian navy, and focusing largely upon our epic internal migrations to the South and the West, such historians have indulged in a kind of hindsight that obscures the true nature of the period. As a result the changes wrought by twentieth-century events have been overly dramatized and the continuities ignored. Twentieth-century historians, immersed in what has been labeled an "Age of Anxiety," have forgotten that nineteenth-century man faced his insecurities too. The contrast perhaps lies in the fact that he faced up to them well, looked beyond himself, and at times left a better world as a result of his adventures. These men of mid-century were men of action and foresight and seldom, as the phrase goes, "sicklied o'er with the pale cast of thought." To them emergent America represented an exciting experiment—an opportunity and a mission to spread the ideals of republicanism, Christianity, and new technology across the world horizon. But to do this, to proselytize and compete, particularly for a country with a miniature army and a lilliputian navy, entailed great risks. It meant constantly facing up to the world's great powers across the tenuous borders of world diplomacy. It was not free in the sense of being without peril and anxieties—a pure "gift of nature," as it were. And it certainly did not represent security.

This book, then, attempts to paint American diplomacy on a large canvas—one suitable to the aspirations of the age. The struggle for Texas and Oregon and the window on the Pacific, the war with Mexico, the postwar adventures and skirmishes in the Caribbean, the penetration of South America and the Far East, the competition for Antarctica and the South Sea islands, and the drawing of the great Pacific border at Hawaii are all parts of the same story of which the American westward movement becomes only the best-known episode. These diplomatic activities were the political and economic representation of the same Humboldtean and romantic vision that inspired the painter Frederick Church

---

[1] For two outstanding statements of this position see C. Vann Woodward, "The Age of Reinterpretation," *The American Historical Review*, LXVI, 1–19 (October 1960), and an earlier work, Ralph H. Gabriel, *The Course of American Democratic Thought* (New York: The Ronald Press Co., 2nd ed., 1956), p. 11.

to do his vast canvases of the heart of the Andes, that sent Captain Wilkes along the fog-shrouded coasts of the Antarctic for 1500 miles in leaky wooden ships, that gave Melville his special vision of the whaling world and the Marquesas, that sent Gibbon and Herndon down the Amazon, Stephens into Yucatan, and Walker, "the grey-eyed man of destiny," into Nicaragua, and the vision and impulse that sent General Scott's tired heroes into the Halls of Montezuma convinced that they were the harbingers of civilization come to light up darkest Mexico. This is to say that diplomacy cannot be divorced from the culture that produces and sustains it. It is so in the twentieth century and it was so in the nineteenth century.

One thing more is relevant: this romantic mid-nineteenth-century impulse for American expansion was not itself a new or original phenomenon. It was only a heightened and more self-conscious expression of what had existed since the birth of the Republic and before that in the colonial experience. Like practically everything else "American," it was borrowed from our European forebears. Britain and France had their "romantic horizon" in the seventeenth and eighteenth centuries led by explorers from Jacques Cartier to Captain Cook and followed by the great merchant companies and the lowly consuls who established outposts from the Levant and the Coromandel Coast to Michlimackinac and Valparaiso. Richard Van Alstyne has astutely dated American imperial aspirations from the French and Indian War, when the colonials first became aware of the vast continental strategy of French containment and British penetration in the struggle for North America.[2] Seen in this context, the strategy of American and French diplomats during the Revolution also becomes a strategy of containment—attempted containment and dismemberment of the British Empire in North America, in the West Indies, and on the high seas. Britain in turn faced France not only over the Channel border but over more subtle borders in the western hemisphere and, at the same time, she attempted then and throughout much

---

[2] Richard W. Van Alstyne: *The Rising American Empire* (New York: Oxford University Press, 1960), pp. 1–28. The present author has been much stimulated throughout the present work by Prof. Van Alstyne's approach in this splendid book.

of the early nineteenth century to encircle and constrict, even to divide, the United States. Spain of course, did likewise in Trans-Appalachia, the valley of the Mississippi, and in the West and Southwest. Thus when America entered the game of global strategy the rules were all laid down, the stakes relatively clear, the precedents set, and the opportunities apparent. Infiltration and internal subversion were virtually the only original American contribution to the technique of worldwide imperialism. These came naturally, one might almost be tempted to say innocently, to a country bent on genuine settlement rather than exploitation and whose rapidly burgeoning and venturesome population had, as Thomas Hart Benton once put it, "not got land enough."

Something of the spirit of the age was caught by Bernard De Voto when he recounted the possibly apocryphal story of John T. Hughes of the First Missouri Mounted Volunteers. Hughes described how a party of Santa Fe traders crossing the prairie looked up just after the passage of a thunderstorm and saw the image of an eagle spread out across the setting sun. They knew then, according to Hughes' account, that "in less than twelve months the eagle of liberty would spread his broad pinions over the plains of the west, and that the flag of our country would wave over the cities of Mexico and Chihuahua."[3]

Likewise something of the objectives of the expansionists was voiced by Zenas Leonard, a member of Joseph Reddeford Walker's weary band of mountain trappers, which had just made its way across the Great Basin and over the high Sierras into California. As he looked out across San Francisco Bay, Leonard wrote:

Much of this vast waste of territory belongs to the Republic of the United States. What a theme to contemplate its settlement and civilization. Will the jurisdiction of the federal government ever succeed in civilizing the thousands of savages now roaming over these plains and her hardy free-born population here plant their homes, build their towns and cities, and say here shall the arts and sciences of civilization take root and flourish?[4]

Back in Washington, Senator Thomas Hart Benton had a more grandiose if more succinct objective. Pointing out beyond the Rocky

---

[3] Quoted in Bernard De Voto: *The Year of Decision* (Boston: Houghton Mifflin Company, 1942), p. 3.

[4] Zenas Leonard: *Narrative of the Adventures of Zenas Leonard Fur Trader* John C. Ewers, ed. (Norman, Okla.: Oklahoma University Press, 1959), pp. 94–95.

Mountains, beyond the shores of the Pacific, he declaimed simply:
"There lies the East, there lies India."[5]

Expansion, yes. Destiny, yes. Republican and democratic settlement, yes. Limits, no. It was an age of ambition—of grand symbols
and dreams and portents and destiny. Young America, appropriately tutored, stood ready to test itself against the powers and
mysteries of the earth. The eagle, indeed, had begun to scream.

---

[5] Quoted in Henry Nash Smith, *Virgin Land, The American West As Symbol and
Myth* (Cambridge, Mass.: Harvard Univ. Press, 1950), pp. 23–24.

CHAPTER I

Clear-Eyed Men of Destiny

THE FOUNDATIONS of American expansionism were laid by two very different men, who nevertheless had much in common—Thomas Jefferson and John Quincy Adams. Jefferson, the Virginian, stood for the agrarian way of life. As a farmer and local politician he believed that "those who till the earth are the chosen people of God."[1] And as a young surveyor, he had traveled in the backcountry enough to learn something of the needs, indeed the demands, of the sturdy Scotch-Irish pioneers who were pushing westward regardless of the dangers and the niceties of national jurisdiction. But the image of Jefferson the simple agrarian can be misleading. He was also a cosmopolite—a romantic child of the eighteenth-century Enlightenment, who had been to France, who had absorbed much of the science and learning of the day, and whose imagination was therefore global. Even in his Revolutionary days his instinct, and that of many of his associates, was to address himself to "a candid world." His friends were veterans of the world's political battlefields—Joseph Priestly, the Marquis de Lafayette, and Tom Paine. Later, following Franklin, he became president of one of the most important world organizations of the time, the American Philosophical Society—modeled successfully on its more famous English counterpart, the Royal Society of London. His house, built atop a mountain in the Virginia wilds, was a Palladian villa with a simulated Roman ruin in the garden. It was the height of fashion and sophistication, but it stood on the edge of a wilderness facing West. Jefferson, therefore, combined the values

---

[1] Thomas Jefferson, "Notes on Virginia," in *The Life and Selected Writings of Thomas Jefferson*, Adrienne Koch and William Peden, eds. (New York: Modern Library Edition, 1944), p. 280.

of the republican and agrarian democrat with the instinct, taste, and knowledge of a man of the world.

John Quincy Adams of Braintree, Massachusetts, has always seemed the more provincial of the two. Adams was almost a caricature of the staunch, introspective New England puritan. He arose before dawn to read his Bible and study his Latin classics, and was dyspeptic throughout the day if, on a rare occasion, he failed to beat the sun. However, he was also a man of the world. From the beginning, thanks to the advantage of being a child of the Revolution and having a presidential, one might say "founding," father, John Quincy Adams was keenly aware of the intricacies and perils of world diplomacy. He was among the first, for example, to note the dangers of prolonging the Revolutionary alliance with France, and at an early age expressed his sentiments in speeches and letters to the editors of various Boston papers, a gesture more effective then than now. In 1794, at the age of 31, he was appointed by Washington as an envoy to the Hague and thus began his long career in the foreign service. He went to Holland, then London, then Prussia, and then to Russia where he secured the friendship and allegiance of the Czar to the American cause. He was one of the negotiators of the Treaty of Ghent ending the War of 1812, and just before becoming Secretary of State under President Monroe, he was Minister to the Court of St. James, the premier position in the American diplomatic service. Therefore, although Adams loved New England—loved it enough to place the plight of codfishermen and poor impressed seamen, and the fortunes of sea otter hunters and whalers uppermost in his mind, he was also a man of the world. He was no stranger to continental and intercontinental strategy. He, too, was a devotee of European science and learning and, like Jefferson, he worked to advance these enterprises in America. He was not an agrarian, however. He represented the maritime interests of New England; but he was enough of a strategist to realize that America's maritime interests could best be served by a policy of continentalism that looked westward to the Pacific. And so, along with Jefferson, he became one of the architects of American westward expansion.

The vision of these two men of the world—the one looking toward development of an inland and democratic empire, the other looking toward eventual command of the sea—became the cornerstone of

American expansionism. They set the pattern, and a daring pattern it was, for the fledgling American empire that flung itself brashly and boldly across the romantic world horizon, and from which to this day there has been no retreat.

I

In the beginning Jefferson did not think of the West as necessarily an American West. Rather, he was impressed with the possibility of generating a series of republics across the continent which would be based on the American model. They would be composed of the same people, with the same values, the same occupations, and the same devotion to democratic and republican principles. Although he had been instrumental in formulating the territorial ordinance of 1785, later to be followed by the more famous Northwest Ordinance of 1787, which provided for eventual entry of new states into the Union on an equal footing with the original thirteen, Jefferson held little hope of holding even the Trans-Appalachian country, whose natural orientation was the Mississippi and New Orleans rather than the Atlantic seaboard. At best he looked forward to the distant day when, with all the sister republics established, a great continental merger might take place—a merger like that of the original thirteen colonies, based on a decent respect for the sovereignty of the individual states.

This outlook, however, did not seriously impair his missionary enthusiasm. He believed that the boundaries of the American republic itself should, if possible, include all of what had once been the British Empire in North America, that is, everything west to the Mississippi and northward to the Arctic Circle. He also hoped to embrace the Spanish Floridas and Cuba as a necessary outpost in the Caribbean. Beyond these limits the gospel of American republicanism knew no bounds. It could stretch westward to the Pacific and southward to Patagonia. Although in his own administration Jefferson relied upon neutrality and the embargo, in 1812 he became a War Hawk.

Various men and events influenced Jefferson's career as an expansionist. In 1785, while in Paris, he met John Ledyard, a former noncommissioned officer under Captain Cook, and Ledyard's description of Cook's Pacific voyages, particularly the new-found strategic and commercial possibilities of the Northwest coast, inspired Jefferson to send Ledyard, in 1787, on a truly global mission across Europe, across the Empire of Russia, and across the Pacific to the remote shores of the Northwest coast of America. No one has explained why Jefferson did not simply employ a ship to carry the explorer to his remote objective. At any rate, Ledyard failed. He was stopped by the Empress of Russia somewhere in Siberia, and sent back to Europe. The end of his grand adventure came in Egypt when he died trying to ascend the Nile.

Another expedition into the western country in 1792 led by the French botanist André Michaux, and designed to be transcontinental, also failed. All the while, however, Jefferson continued to receive reports, maps, and rumors of the success of the Canadian Northwest Company in its plans for expansion west to the Pacific. The crossing of the continent by Alexander Mackenzie in 1793 was an important first step that aroused Jefferson's anxiety. If the Canadian Northwest Company could build on the old French line of communication via the lakes and carry this westward beyond the "Stony Mountains," it might become possessor of the fabled Northwest Passage and hence master of the entire western half of North America. In that event Canada would indeed be lost to the United States, and the American empire severely circumscribed.

In addition to these aggressive English activities, Jefferson also had to be concerned with Spain. Spanish officials had closed the Mississippi to American commerce and were using their control of the river not only to block American expansion to the Southwest but also as a means of seducing the allegiance of the Trans-Appalachian settlers away from the United States. It was the stick and the carrot. No western commerce was possible with the Mississippi closed. On the other hand, if the western settlers would affiliate with Spain, the rich commerce of the Mississippi would be theirs from St. Louis to New Orleans and beyond to the Caribbean and Europe. If, as was once observed, Florida was "a pistol pointed at the heart of the United States," then control of the mouth of the Mississippi was a cannon that could blow the infant republic to pieces.

In 1802, spurred on by his fears of British and Spanish operations in the West, and before the United States had any legitimate claim to the territory, Jefferson resolved to make a reconnaissance of the unknown western country from the Mississippi to the Pacific. Although in a conversation with the Spanish Ambassador, Jefferson termed his proposed expedition, "a literary or scientific enterprise," actually his plans were more ambitious. They involved not only serious scientific collecting, but three further objectives: first, to seek out a possible northwest passage to the Pacific; second, to establish an American sphere of influence among the Indians and a claim by exploration to the western country that would limit British expansionism; and third, to explore the possibilities for trade and commerce with the tribes of the Far West. It was the last of these that he stressed in his message to Congress, on January 18, 1803, which asked for funds to finance the expedition. He concealed not only his more ambitious diplomatic objectives but also his serious scientific aims and concentrated on the idea of commerce because this function was well within his powers as President. The other purposes would have raised certain opposition among his enemies in Congress, who were extreme strict constructionists and inclined to be reserved when it came to ambitious plans for expansion that threatened to dilute the original Union. In any case Jefferson got his appropriation, some $5000, and the Lewis and Clark enterprise, after a period of intensive training for the two explorers, got under way, headed for a reconnaissance of what was technically claimed and recognized as Spanish territory. Clearly the Lewis and Clark expedition represented a prime diplomatic weapon in the struggle for a continent.

That the Spanish recognized it as such is also clear. Although the Spanish Ambassador gave cautious assent to Jefferson's proposal, he was soon sending out dispatches to Spain and the Spanish governors in New Orleans and Santa Fe that raised alarm over the Lewis and Clark intrusion into Spanish territory. While Lewis and Clark were ascending the Missouri River in 1804, the Spanish governor in Santa Fe launched several expeditions northward toward the Missouri in a futile effort to turn them back. Therefore, although the Lewis and Clark expedition succeeded admirably in all its objectives in the Northwest, even establishing a temporary settlement at Fort Clatsop, near the mouth of the Columbia, it also succeeded in bolstering Spanish and British efforts to prevent Americans from gaining a significant foothold west of the Mississippi.

The Lewis and Clark expedition, however, had a marked if not curious effect upon American thinking about the Far West. Their hazardous trip across the mountains and down the Columbia River indicated that no easy passage by water to the Pacific existed, at least in the Northwest. Thus the idea of the passage to India was severely circumscribed. But when the reports of their trek began to be published, notably in Patrick Gass's journal in 1809, the importance of the interior trade of the mountains and the Columbia became obvious. Thus the same elements which had continually urged the federal government to drive the British traders out of the near Northwest (Michigan, Wisconsin, Iowa, Minnesota, and the Dakotas) and to maintain control over the fur trade area below the 49th parallel from Lake of the Woods to the Rocky Mountains, arose with a new enthusiasm to demand control of the far Northwest. This was a bit ambitious for Jefferson's time, since not until after the Treaty of Ghent in 1815 were the British held back in any significant way from controlling even the near Northwest and hence the strategic sources of the Mississippi. As late as 1821 the Canadian Red River settlements were a wedge driven deep into America's western ambitions. Nevertheless, the Lewis and Clark expedition called attention to the commercial riches that control of the Northwest might bring, inspired a new determination to wrest control of that territory from the British, and focused the primary attention of American expansionists for a time upon the continental interior.

Jefferson's ultimate master stroke as an expansionist was, of course, the Louisiana Purchase. The Mississippi, key to all the western country beyond the Appalachians, provided a formidable diplomatic weapon to whoever controlled it. Spain itself recognized this fact and clung tenaciously to a string of outposts from New Orleans to St. Louis, patrolling the great river by means of a picturesque fleet of galleys and galleons. From time to time she offered special concessions to western settlers in an effort to detach them from the Union, and once, in the case of Kentucky, she very nearly succeeded through the efforts of James Wilkinson. By the Treaty of San Lorenzo in 1795, however, Spain lessened tensions somewhat by guaranteeing Americans the right to navigate the Mississippi and the right of deposit at New Orleans. This right, nonetheless, was subject to a series of tedious qualifications that made traffic on the Mississippi still a very risky venture. There was only one conclusion—the Mississippi, particularly its mouth at New Orleans, in the control of a foreign power would always be a direct threat to the United States.

The threat became even more direct with the arousal of French interest in Louisiana. In 1796, General Collot of the French army made a trip down the Ohio and the Mississippi mapping the river country in preparation for what could only be interpreted as a future military campaign in that region. Further fears were aroused when the Spanish Intendant at New Orleans, on July 14, 1802, on direct order from Spain, and in violation of Pinckney's Treaty, closed the port of New Orleans to American trade. Meanwhile rumors of a secret treaty retroceding Louisiana from Spain to France circulated throughout Europe and America, making Collot's expedition all the more ominous.

It was not until 1802 that Jefferson learned that such a treaty had actually been completed—on October 1, 1800, at San Ildefonso —and that Napoleon Bonaparte was now master of Louisiana and the Mississippi. Jefferson did not know, but he could guess that Bonaparte had great plans for his new American possessions which made them even more of a threat to American security. Actually Napoleon planned a western hemisphere project that pivoted on New Orleans in which raw materials would be drawn from Louisiana and used to build up trade with the French islands in the West Indies. To facilitate this plan, in 1801 he sent General LeClerc to reconquer Santo Domingo and the sugar islands, and he made plans to reinforce the New Orleans and Mississippi outposts.

In the face of this news Jefferson remained relatively undisturbed for a time, since he believed that war in Europe was imminent, and when it came, the United States would be able to acquire New Orleans without difficulty. He had Robert Livingston in Paris working to persuade Napoleon to cede New Orleans to the United States. And he attempted to play on French fear of the English by sending his friend Du Pont de Nemours to Paris with letters suggesting that, if France did not cede New Orleans to the United States, an English alliance might become advisable. Jefferson's casual diplomacy was accelerated, however, by several factors. First, the campaign in Santo Domingo and the reinforcement of New Orleans made Bonaparte's aggressive plans apparent. Second, the closing of the Mississippi provided an explosive issue for his political opponents at home, creating a natural alliance between the Westerners and the New England Federalists, who greatly feared France's threat to the Union. Jefferson's hand was forced. As Professor Samuel Flagg Bemis has put it so dramatically:

This presented the most serious menace to the territorial integrity of the United States since its independence had been established. . . . Napoleon Bonaparte became Thomas Jefferson's terrible problem.[2]

Jefferson responded by sending Monroe to France on March 8, 1803, with orders to try to purchase New Orleans and the Floridas for $6 million. It was a desperate measure.

Meanwhile, however, Robert Livingston had been carefully negotiating with the French minister Talleyrand, and in so doing had conceived the idea of purchasing all of what had once been French Louisiana, including New Orleans. His argument was that in American hands it would be a buffer against further British encroachment through Canada upon the French empire in the western hemisphere. It was a thin argument at the time, but it came to have merit as events in Europe and the West Indies rapidly altered Napoleon's plans.

In order for Napoleon's western hemisphere project to succeed, peace was needed in Europe, and the conquest of the West Indies had to proceed rapidly. Neither occurred. Fifty-thousand French soldiers died of fever in Santo Domingo, and ice blocked plans for sending reinforcements from Holland. The Peace of Amiens began to crumble as Napoleon moved into Holland, Italy, and Switzerland, while England made plans for war. Stabilizing the conditions in Europe commanded the Emperor's primary attention, and Louisiana became not only a distraction but a possible hostage to England in the event of a continental war. Hence in April of 1803 Talleyrand suddenly proposed to Livingston the sale of all of French Louisiana to the United States. When Monroe arrived in Paris the details of a treaty were worked out. The United States bought Louisiana, which was defined as:

---

[2] Samuel Flagg Bemis, *A Diplomatic History of the United States*, 3rd ed. (New York: Holt, Rinehart and Winston Co., 1965), p. 129.

Louisiana with the Same extent that it now has in the hands of Spain, and that it had when France possessed it; and Such as it Should be after the Treaties subsequently entered into between Spain and other States.[3]

The treaty was signed on April 30, 1803, and the cost was f60 million, plus the assumption of United States claims up to f20 million or $15 million. This purchase, negotiated by Livingston and Monroe, and sanctioned by Jefferson, had two inestimable advantages. It saved the Union by removing the danger of French or Spanish use of the Mississippi to drive a wedge into the western country. And it provided America with an inland empire that more than doubled the original size of the country, bringing with it rich natural resources, a path of inland commerce, and a springboard for extending America across to the Pacific along the route traced by Lewis and Clark. A few years after the purchase, Jefferson confirmed his interest in this latter objective by encouraging the fur merchant John Jacob Astor to establish his trading post, Fort Astoria, at the mouth of the Columbia River, whence it was hoped he could dominate the inland trade of the West, the Pacific Coast sea otter trade, and the trans-Pacific trade with China. Out of Astor's enterprise might come the first of those sister republics friendly to the United States that would consummate the mission of the North American people, and incidentally hold back the territorial aspirations of the British in Canada.

Although the acquisition of Louisiana was a master stroke for American continental diplomacy, it nevertheless raised serious problems which remained to be solved in the future. It forecast the dispersion of people and energies over a vast territory which, through lack of communications, would be but loosely held. "We rush like a comet into infinite space" wailed the Federalist Fisher Ames with this very danger in mind.[4]

In addition to the dispersion and disunity that might result, possession of Louisiana inevitably brought the United States once again into direct confrontation with Spain and, more importantly,

---

[3] Quoted in *Ibid.*, p. 136.
[4] Quoted in David M. Potter and Thomas Manning, *Nationalism and Sectionalism in America 1775–1877* (New York: Henry Holt & Co., 1949), p. 69.

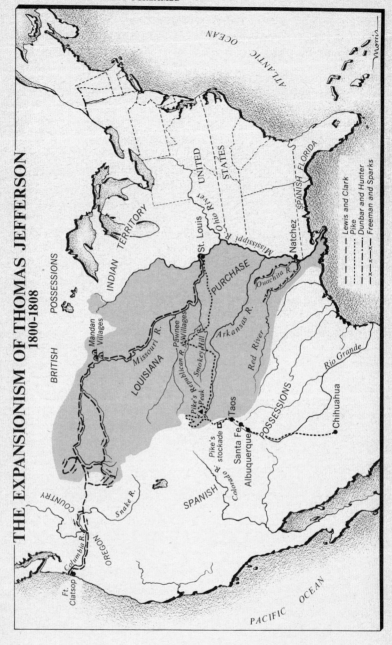

THE EXPANSIONISM OF THOMAS JEFFERSON
1800-1808

with England, the most powerful nation on earth. These twin confrontations drew the perilous lines of continental diplomacy virtually until mid-century.

II

The burden of these later anxieties was assumed by the gentleman from Braintree, John Quincy Adams. In the course of his career he was to extend American continental commitments even farther, and although he was successful, he did nothing to lessen the tensions between the United States and its two powerful rivals. When Adams assumed his post as Secretary of State he faced several severe problems which related to the question of expansion. To begin with, according to the agreement signed at Ghent, all territories seized by the British or the Americans were to revert back to their *status quo ante bellum.* In the Northwest this presented a particularly acute problem for during the war Canada had moved south. British agents and traders controlled virtually the entire near Northwest, and it was only through the valiant efforts of Manuel Lisa, the St. Louis fur trader, who mobilized the Sioux against them on the Upper Missouri, that the British were not able to move south as far as St. Louis. In the far Northwest, Astoria had fallen to a ragtag and bobtail brigade of Northwest Company men who came out of the woods and down the Columbia to demand its surrender. Fearing British military conquest, the Astoria partners had sold Astoria to the Northwest Company. But since this was a private commercial venture they had no right to bargain away American political claims to the Columbia region and they did not do so. Sometime later when the British Man-of-War H.M.S. *Raccoon* put in at Astoria, its commander found to his dismay that the fort was already in British hands and he could not have the "glory" of capturing it. So he contented himself with raising the Union Jack and sailing away. However, by the Treaty of Ghent, Astoria should properly have been returned to the United States, and the near Northwest cleared of British officials. Adams helped to accomplish these two things.

Albert Gallatin and Richard Rush, the two men sent in 1818 to negotiate with England concerning these and numerous other postwar difficulties, such as impressment of sailors and the Newfoundland fishing rights, under Adams' orders also held fast to the northern boundary line of the 49th parallel from the Lake of the Woods to the crest of the Rockies, thus denying British traders the easy access to the Missouri and the Mississippi which they once enjoyed. A short while before this, out in St. Louis, William Clark, the Governor of Louisiana, began the practice of licensing would-be fur traders, which was an on-the-spot means of excluding Canadian competition. Earlier, in 1795, the federal government had established a group of government-owned trading posts in the region to assert federal control over the Indian trade—a measure that proved somewhat ineffective. In addition, however, after Major Stephen Long surveyed a series of frontier defense posts, John C. Calhoun, the Secretary of War, began planning what came to be called the Yellowstone Expedition. It was to be an expedition in force up the Missouri River which would establish a strategic military outpost at the mouth of the Yellowstone River on the upper Missouri. Although this expedition ultimately proved to be a dismal failure, rumors of an American show of strength in the North Country undoubtedly helped to expedite the agreements of 1818.

On the political front the enthusiasm of the American, if not the British, negotiators was also spurred by the series of articles published by the young western politician, Thomas Hart Benton, in the St. Louis *Enquirer.* Benton, speaking for the St. Louis fur trade interests, for John Floyd of Virginia, and for a number of western-minded men, demanded that the United States government do something about the upper-Missouri situation, and also take steps to acquire Oregon. Following Jefferson, as he did most of his life, Benton felt that the United States could probably not extend its sovereignty to Oregon—indeed he pictured the "fabled god Terminus" astride the Rocky Mountains preventing future mass migrations in that direction—but he saw Oregon and the Columbia as a strategic trading outpost on the road to India: hence of supreme importance to American interests. A settlement of republican-minded emigrants from the United States at the mouth of the Columbia would give the new nation a window on the Pacific, keep the British out, and make the Columbia, and what came to be the Oregon Trail (discovered by Robert Stuart in 1813) a vital path of inland commerce between the Mississippi

Valley and the Pacific with its sea otter and China trade. Benton's grandiose rhetoric in defense of this aggressive plan more than matched the audacity of the plan itself, which had once been the dream of John Jacob Astor and of Thomas Jefferson.

Given these pressures, the results of the negotiations of 1818 were at least satisfactory. No boundary west of the Rocky Mountains was agreed upon. In August, 1818, Astoria was returned to American sovereignty and an official American claim was established north of the Columbia River, although it took a warship, the U.S.S. *Ontario*, to do it. And finally the negotiators agreed to a joint occupation treaty to extend for ten years which left both the British and Americans free to trade in the Oregon country, but which did not prejudice the claims of either nation to political sovereignty over the region. Spanish interests in the Northwest were for the time being ignored.

Adams was not, however, unmindful of Spain. The object of his immediate attention was Florida, both East Florida, "the pistol pointed at the heart of the United States," and West Florida, the region extending from the Mississippi to the present-day Florida line. The latter, Spain claimed, was not properly part of the Louisiana Purchase, and the former, though she held it loosely under tolerance from the Indians, she regarded as having great strategic if not sentimental value. Both of these areas were troublesome to the United States because from them, spurred on by British and Spanish soldiers of fortune and agents of the Panton-Leslie Company, bands of brigands, red men and white, terrorized settlements on the American southwestern frontier. It fell to Adams to extinguish these conflagrations by acquiring the Floridas by any peaceful means possible. In performing this task he had powerful aid from his future lifelong political antagonist, General Andrew Jackson.

Under Monroe's orders Jackson employed the doctrine of "hot pursuit" and invaded Florida, capturing Pensacola and St. Mark's. There, with 3,000 men he chastised the Indians, humiliated the Spanish officials, and precipitated a serious international crisis by executing two British filibusters, Armbrister and Arbuthnot— one by hanging and the other by the firing squad. Weak-minded, vindictive or politically opportunistic members of Monroe's cabinet wished to disavow or publicly condemn Jackson's actions.

But Adams persuaded Monroe against this action, despite the possibility of war with England and Spain. This course proved to be an expedient one. Lord Castlereagh and the British negotiators in London acknowledged the justice of Jackson's actions and proceeded in good spirits to negotiate the other issues of the treaty of 1818. Spain, on the other hand, although she protested vehemently, saw clearly that the Floridas were beyond her practical control. This increased her willingness to trade them for some more secure piece of property, in point of fact Texas, and if possible the entire Trans-Mississippi West, as far north as the upper Missouri.

Adams' negotiation of the transcontinental boundary treaty of 1819 thus began as a swap: Texas (whatever that was) for the Floridas. As a student of history, Adams could not help being aware of Spain's insecurity over Texas and New Mexico. In 1806, Zebulon Pike was captured on the upper Rio Grande and held prisoner, his papers and maps were confiscated, and he was summarily sent back to the United States by the quickest possible route. Shortly afterward, in 1807, Captains Freeman and Sparks were turned back on the Red River. That same year the fur trader Anthony Glass was repeatedly threatened by Spanish authorities as he intruded on what they regarded as their territory. An 1812 trading expedition by Robert McKnight to Santa Fe landed him in a Chihuahua prison for nine years. The Gutierrez-Magee filibustering expedition into Texas in 1813 was put down and its leaders executed. In 1818 the fur trader Auguste Chouteau and his partner Jules De Mun were captured on the upper Arkansas. Their furs were confiscated; they were forced to kneel and kiss the document sentencing them; and then they were sent home with a bare minimum of equipment. These were convincing demonstrations of Spanish insecurities regarding Texas, but what made them seem outrageous to the United States was the fact that, if the limits of the Louisiana Purchase included the watershed of the Mississippi, then the territory to the headwaters of the Arkansas and Red Rivers belonged to the United States. Indeed, certain enthusiasts with a poor knowledge of geography claimed even the Rio Grande on this basis.

Needless to say, faced by a threatened American penetration of its territories, Spain, by 1819, was ready to negotiate a boundary that would give her a buffer against American invasion. Though Adams never knew it, she was willing to retreat all the way to the Rio Grande.

The negotiations with the Spanish minister Onis, a harried but tenacious diplomat, who awoke one morning to find a dead chicken tied to his doorbell rope, began with Adams offering a Texas boundary and indemnity for the Floridas. The Spanish sought a larger buffer to the West, however, and attempted to extend the Texas border from the high point of land between two creeks near Natchitoches, Louisiana, north to the Missouri River. In this way they could acquire most of Louisiana in exchange for the Floridas, which they could not hold in any case. This strategy, however, caused Adams to revise his own thinking. Previously he had been concerned with southern and southwestern problems; now the vision of a continental empire arose, and he shifted ground. If in exchange for Texas he could acquire the Floridas and also an extension of Louisiana in a wide swath to the Pacific, he would have opened the way to an American empire on the Pacific and gained the key to the continent.

Thus began a series of new negotiations, with the implied threat of an American invasion of the Floridas and Texas hanging in the background. On July 16 Adams, using Melish's inaccurate map of 1818, offered a line up the Colorado River of Texas to the Red River, and then across from the Red River to the crest of the Rocky Mountains, thence along the 41st parallel to the Pacific. Onis countered with a line northward from Natchitoches to the Missouri, then along the Missouri to its headwaters at the Three Forks, the line west from there not specified. And so the negotiations went throughout the fall and winter of 1818-1819, with Onis trying ultimately to get a Missouri-Columbia line to the Pacific with rights of trade on these rivers, and Adams stumping for the Colorado River of Texas or the Sabine River and the 41st parallel. Even an ultimatum offer of October 31, 1818, made at the behest of President Monroe, who had grown impatient, failed to impress Onis. Then Monroe began to give ground and seemed almost inclined to accept Onis' proposal of February 1, 1819, which was a line up the Arkansas River to the mythical San Clemente River, to the 43rd parallel and along it to the sea. But Adams held firm, and eventually on February 22, 1819, he had his transcontinental boundary treaty. The major provisions of the treaty included the Spanish cession of the Floridas, East and West, to the United States, the assumption by the United States of American claims against Spain up to $5 million, and a western boundary line which began at the mouth of the Sabine River, continued north along the western bank of that river to the 32nd parallel of latitude, thence by a line due north to the Red River, thence westward up the south bank of the Red River to the 100th meridian of longitude, thence across the Red River due north on the 100th meridian to the south bank of the Arkansas River, thence up that river to its source in latitude 42° north, and westward from that point along the 42nd parallel to the Pacific, as laid down in Melish's map of 1818.

Adams had thus bartered away Texas, but he had gained the Floridas and, equally important, he had gained his coveted trans-continental corridor to the Pacific. In accomplishing this he had served the New England sea traders well. But, in addition, despite much western opposition, he had served the West equally well since the acquisition of the Spanish claims to the Northwest opened the way for the development of the Rocky Mountain fur trade. However, Westerners fretted that he had given up Texas and the potential riches of the Southwest. Present-day knowledge of Spanish documents indicates that he had indeed done so. But Adams could not have known this at the time, and thus he did the best he could. As his biographer remarks,

Even without Texas the Transcontinental Treaty with Spain was the great-est diplomatic victory won by any single individual in the history of the United States.[5]

III

One further course of diplomatic events that took place while Adams was Secretary of State continued—indeed exaggerated—the emergence of America on the horizon of world diplomacy. This involved the development or formulation of an American policy for the entire western hemisphere that culminated in the Monroe Doctrine.

---

[5] Samuel Flagg Bemis, *John Quincy Adams and the Foundations of American For-eign Policy* (New York: Alfred A. Knopf Inc., 1956), p. 340.

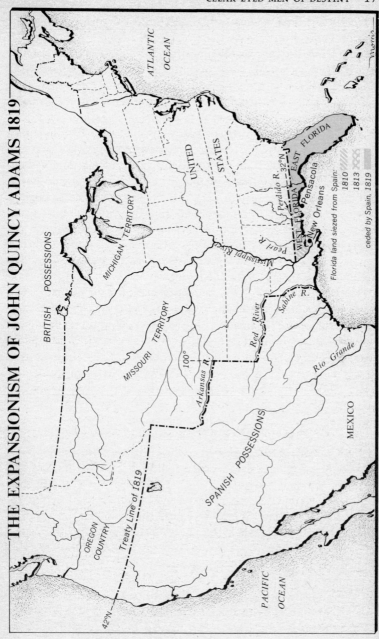

THE EXPANSIONISM OF JOHN QUINCY ADAMS 1819

During the time Adams was negotiating with Spain, the countries of Latin America, encouraged by tradesmen from England and the United States, revolted against Spain, and in a long series of civil wars succeeded in establishing a de facto independence. Since the delicate negotiations with Spain were in progress, Adams was reluctant to recognize the new revolutionary nations although, like Jefferson, he sympathized with their desire for independence. As a New Englander, however, Adams also deplored the outfitting by the new countries of privateers which preyed on world shipping, including that of neutrals. He stood for the principle of freedom of the seas, and the violation of that principle by any power, however just its cause, threatened the principle itself. At least during the Spanish treaty negotiations the canny Braintree moralist used this as an argument to counter the enthusiastic trumpetings of Henry Clay, who was demanding immediate recognition of the new republics, partly out of sincerity and partly because of a desire to embarrass the Monroe administration.

Eventually the new Latin republics ceased their privateering. American business representatives were established in the major ports. And, in 1821, Spain ratified the transcontinental treaty. Between 1822 and 1826 the United States recognized the independence of the seven new Latin American countries, although not all of them were republics patterned after the Jeffersonian democratic model. The United States was the first major nation to recognize formally the independence of the Latin states, and she did so at the risk of offending the major powers of Europe.

After the defeat of Napoleon, the chief continental powers led by the Czar of Russia formed the Holy Alliance with the avowed purpose of keeping peace in Europe through pacts of mutual assistance. Although we now know that there was little chance of a continental nation coming to the aid of Spain in her attempt to regain her lost New World colonies, this did not necessarily appear to be the case when the United States extended its recognition. Rather than a feat of diplomatic daring, however, the recognition of the Latin states appears to have been a response to demands by American trading and maritime interests for official government support in their competition with Britain for the trade of South and Central America.

While these events were occurring, Adams faced still another challenge to his dream of a continental empire. In 1816 the Russians had landed at Bodega Bay north of San Francisco and established a colony, Fort Ross. Subsequently Russia claimed all of the Pacific coast from Alaska to the latitude of Fort Ross, which of course encompassed the newly won Spanish claims above the 42nd parallel. Adams sternly rebuked the Russian expansionists in a note which was later to become the model for the Monroe Doctrine. He wrote to the Russian minister in Washington that the United States contested the right of Russia to her coastal claims, and furthermore he declared, "We should assume distinctly the principle that the American continents are no longer subjects for any new European colonial establishments."⁶ Russia retreated from her untenable and unprofitable position in the face of opposition not only from the United States but also from Britain, and in 1824 concluded a treaty with the United States limiting her territorial aspirations to 54°40′, the present Alaskan boundary. In 1825 a similar treaty with Britain was consummated. Adams had forestalled still another threat by a major power, although the United States had no way of defending her position by anything like the force of arms.

The Monroe Doctrine grew out of this anti-European position. Interested in maintaining good trade relations with South America, the British Minister, George Canning, proposed in 1823 that the United States join with England in making a declaration against any further attempts by the continental powers to colonize the New World. At Adams' insistence Monroe refused to join the British plan. Instead he issued an independent American statement, since known as the Monroe Doctrine, although Adams claimed to be its primary author. The Monroe Doctrine declared:

(1) That the United States did not wish to take part in the politics or wars of Europe.

(2) That the United States would regard as manifestations of an unfriendly disposition to itself the effort of any European power to interfere with the political system of the American continents, or to acquire any new territory on these continents.

The Monroe Doctrine, at first hailed by the new countries of Latin America, now much maligned by the same countries and

⁶ *Ibid.*, p. 368.

transgressed by Soviet intrusions into the Caribbean, was something more and something less than tradition has made it seem. Enforcement of the doctrine depended, of course, in the main, on the British fleet, and in this sense many have considered it a hollow gesture although it was a true commitment. Later generations have seen it as a weapon or facade behind which the United States was able to interfere unduly in the internal affairs of its neighbors, and it has also on occasion served this purpose. Still others regard it as one more inflexible American principle that by its unyielding quality has limited American maneuverability in Latin American affairs, and this is certainly correct. But understood in the context of its own day, the Monroe Doctrine would appear to have several other legitimate purposes. First, it was a refusal to allow Latin America to become exclusively a British protectorate. Second, it reinforced American trading interests in the hemisphere. Third, it announced America's emergence as a power among nations that had to be reckoned with. Fourth, it was a gesture of genuine goodwill and concern for the new Latin republics. Fifth, it was a continual renunciation of European political alliances and a strategic refusal to play the balance-of-power game on Britain's terms. And finally, it was a rallying cry, a nationalistic symbol for Americans at home, that drew the nation together in terms of its ultimate ideals of republican democracy for all. Only the fact of slavery beclouded the lofty pretensions of such a democratic mission.

By the time Adams became president, the United States had acquired a continental empire of its own that looked both inward and outward, south toward the Caribbean, and west toward China and the Pacific. It had, moreover, taken an important place in the world family of nations and, following Jefferson's prophecy, it had spawned sister republics based on the American model as far as Cape Horn. The French had been ousted from North America, and the British, Spanish, and Russians severely circumscribed. This was not the work of a nation that sought or needed a comfortable security. It was the missionary impulse of individuals who had fought their way to freedom and independence, and therefore appreciated their virtues, an impulse making itself felt for the first time around the world.

CHAPTER II

"Will You Come to the Bower . . . ?"

Mexico successfully revolted against Spain in 1821, and within seven months of the establishment of its independence, the United States formally recognized her. As a new nation, Mexico inherited all of the many problems that had formerly plagued the Spanish Empire. Among them was the problem of controlling its extensive imperial holdings to the north—country that had once been termed the "Rim of Christendom." These territories included present day Texas, New Mexico, Colorado, Utah, Nevada, Arizona, and California. In 1821 all of them were held but scarcely controlled by the disorganized Mexican government.

When he ascended to the presidency of the United States, and before his transcontinental boundary treaty was even formally ratified by the Mexican government, John Quincy Adams began to regret his decision to abandon Texas to Spain. Accordingly he sent Joel Poinsett, a South Carolinian experienced in the ways of Latin American diplomacy as his Minister to Mexico in 1825. Poinsett's instructions, written by Henry Clay, were to purchase as much of Texas as he could from Mexico, as far as the Rio Grande if possible, with the purchase price depending on which river—the Pecos, the Colorado, the Brazos, and so forth—the Mexicans would agree to retreat to. Poinsett, something of a scholar, had a certain charm, especially among his fellow diplomats, and a thorough grasp of the emergent-nation mentality. Moreover, the American offer stood a chance of acceptance if it could be put forward as part of the boundary adjustment of the 1819 treaty. However, Poinsett overextended himself and began intriguing in Mexican politics. His purchase offer was refused, in-

21

deed scorned, by the Mexican foreign minister, who in turn offered to purchase from the United States all the land between the Sabine and the Mississippi, though it is not certain what he proposed to use as funds. Poinsett's efforts, therefore, came to naught. Eventually he was declared persona non grata in Mexico and sailed for home.

Andrew Jackson, too, cast a covetous eye on Texas, and his Minister to Mexico, Anthony Butler, a thorough scoundrel, attempted without Jackson's authorization to bribe Mexican officials to sell Texas. In terms of American continental diplomacy, however, Butler's mission to Mexico was more interesting than that of Poinsett. He was authorized by Jackson to offer any amount for a new boundary line running up the Rio Grande to the 37th parallel and then across to the Pacific. Adams and Jefferson had both been transcontinentalists. Jackson followed their logic with even greater enthusiasm. His objective was not only to procure Texas and a large slice of far western territory, but he also wished to secure the ports of Monterey and San Francisco Bay. As such he was the first American president to make the California ports on the Pacific an objective of American continental diplomacy.

What influenced Jackson, the spokesman for western agrarian interests, to focus on this maritime objective? The historian, Norman Graebner, has recently pointed to the reports of the French explorer Eugene Du Flot de Mofrás, who sailed in 1839, or Captain Charles Wilkes, whose expedition to the Northwest coast did not return until 1841, as the major inspirers of an American policy aimed at acquiring a port on the Pacific.[1] However, they came too late to inspire Jackson, and even his own personal representative William A. Slacum, who sailed to the coast during this period, did not report until 1837. Lacking any official reports on the region, Jackson must have gained his interest and information from skippers returning from the cattle-hide trade in California, or quite possibly from a report delivered by Captain Benjamin Bonneville, whose lieutenant, the mountain man Joseph Reddeford Walker, had crossed over the Sierras to San Francisco Bay in 1833. That the future possibilities of San Francisco Bay were "in the air" is indicated by the statement of Zenas Leonard, one of the more

[1] See especially Norman Graebner, *Empire on the Pacific, A Study in American Continental Expansion* (New York: The Ronald Press Co., 1955).

literate trappers who accompanied Walker's expedition and whose remarks are quoted in the introduction to this work. Leonard published this statement in 1838, but Bonneville, his employer, an unofficial agent of the United States government, may have passed on this information somewhat earlier, although concrete evidence of this fact is lacking. It is known, however, that when he returned from the West, Bonneville presented the War Department with all his journals and maps. And at the Senate inquiry, concerning his reinstatement in the regular army, Bonneville insisted that he had forwarded two reports of his activities and discoveries to the War Department, although only one, his first report of July 29, 1833, was ever found.[2] At any rate, President Jackson interjected a shrewd note into American expansionist policy when he sought to purchase California's two major ports. This was to no avail, however, and although Butler continued his nefarious activities in Mexico for seven years, he only succeeded in worsening Mexican-American relations.

American concern (often attributed to greed or "agrarian cupidity") for the acquisition of Texas and California during and after the Jackson administration might justifiably be ascribed to an American apprehension that these loosely held provinces might fall into British or French hands. Although the researches of Ephraim D. Adams indicate that England had no serious design on either of these two territories,[3] American policymakers had no way of being certain of this, and they had much in the way of precedent, recounted earlier, to cause their fears. If Britain or France did not intend seizure of the derelict provinces of Texas and California over the question of claims, they nevertheless made efforts to secure the independence of these provinces with the intention of creating potential rivals on the North American continent that would compete with American planters and traders and circumscribe American westward development.[4] Any conscientious president must necessarily have been alert to the time-

---

[2] See Bonneville File, R. G. 46, National Archives. Also see Washington Irving, *The Adventures of Captain Bonneville*, Edgely Todd, ed. (Norman, Okla.: University of Oklahoma Press, 1961), Introduction.
[3] See Ephraim D. Adams, *British Interests and Activities in Texas, 1838–1896* (Baltimore: Johns Hopkins Press, 1910).
[4] *Ibid.*, passim.

worn imperial strategies of containment and balance of power, whose shadows were cast over the Caribbean and the Pacific by the two great maritime powers of the world.

Hence it would appear that the motivation for American continental expansion was more complex than simple greed. It was compounded of agrarian cupidity, but it also included equal parts of mission, in the idealistic sense; simple romanticism; the desire for trade; racial prejudice; a sense of outrage at not being able to control politically territory that had been explored, populated, and settled by Americans at great cost of blood and treasure; and finally, perhaps most of all, a basic sense of insecurity felt by a still youthful republic confronting formidable rivals. It was an insecurity glossed over by the vaguely satisfying, exaggerated jingoistic slogans of the day best represented by that ringing but hollow phrase—Manifest Destiny.

I

While Adams and Jackson were attempting to secure parts of Mexico for the United States, other Americans were fulfilling the more innocent but subtle prophecy of Jefferson. They were going to Texas, where they would eventually establish one of those "sister republics" that in due course would affiliate with the Union. Although it was not their plan at the time, the migration of Americans into Texas represented one of the most successful examples in all history of what might today be called "infiltration and subversion." It was an American innovation pursued more deliberately in Oregon than in Texas, but the Mexican government failed to see the distinction. Mexico, a new nation suffering from an even greater insecurity than the United States, saw the events culminating in the Texan Revolution as a betrayal—a betrayal of the initial gestures of friendship and grants of land given to refugee settlers, and a betrayal of American protestations of neutrality. This made for a heightened hostility that led to war.

Immediately after the Mexican revolution against Spain, the Mexican policy vis-à-vis the United States was one of distinct friendship. Santa Fe, once so closely guarded against American traders, was thrown open to commerce, and after William Becknell laid out the Santa Fe Trail in 1821 the southwestern road to New Mexico became for a time one of the richest paths of inland commerce. It made St. Louis, Westport, and Independence prosperous outposts of western trade.

Also, Mexico, seeking to populate and develop Texas, began granting land to settlers from the United States. Moses Austin, originally from Durham, Connecticut but more recently a citizen of Missouri, secured the first large grant from the Mexican government on January 19, 1821. He was to serve as *empresario* and bring in three-hundred American families to settle a tract of land along the lower Brazos River. On his return to Missouri, Moses Austin died and the Texas project was taken up by his son, Stephen F. Austin. When Austin returned to Texas with his first settlers in 1822, he found that his father's grant had been revoked because of another revolution in Mexico, but eventually, in 1823, it was restored. After 1823 large numbers of settlers poured into Texas, overland and by sea, driven west by the rising prices of public land in the United States. By the end of 1824 some 272 family land titles had been granted. Soon other promoters began to bring in settlers. Austin acquired a partner, Samuel May Williams. Green DeWitt established a colony along the Lavaca and Guadalupe rivers. Hayden Edwards brought people into an east Texas settlement. David G. Burnet, Lorenzo de Zavala, Joseph Vehlein, Arthur Wavell, Sterling C. Robertson, and Benjamin Milam all became *empresarios* with sizeable grants of land. John McMullen and James McGloin, residents of Matamoros, even managed to settle their tracts with families from Ireland.

The conditions imposed on these settlers were that they must become citizens of Mexico, must actually develop the land within a specified period of time, must adopt the Catholic religion, and must obey the laws and duly constituted governmental officials. The latter conditions were generally specified and authorized by the Mexican Constitution of 1824. After 1825 Texas was affiliated with Coahuila and the capital of the province was located in Saltillo, though it later shifted to Monclova.

From the beginning, although there were great cultural differences and adjustments to be made (particularly in matters of religion and law), relations between Mexican officials and the settlers were good. The Texans nominally accepted the Catholic faith and Mexican officials seemed not unduly concerned in any case, since there were few priests in the province. The question of law, however, caused some difficulty. Mexican law did not derive from the Anglo-Saxon democratic tradition in which the individual was basically more important than the State. Instead, it derived from Roman and Spanish law. Authority was from the top downward. Titles to land were privileges, grants by the State. Private property was not an inherent right. Laws were made by judges. There was no trial by jury, and in Texas even trivial matters had to be settled by lengthy correspondence and written decisions stemming from the court at Saltillo—causing great hardship. Moreover, representation in the provincial assembly was not guaranteed, nor was it proportional. Texas had one representative, ultimately three.

In general, looking at both Texas and New Mexico of the period, it must be said that the people scarcely lived under a government of law in the commonly accepted sense of the word. Rather it was government by men—appointed officials—which, given the continual revolutionary turmoil in Mexico and the constant turnover of public officials, meant that it was government by individual whim or caprice that often used statutes or proclamations to give personal fancies the semblance of legal authority and justice. Perhaps this explains the tremendous avalanche of broadsides and proclamations that rolled off Mexican presses during the critical period, 1821 to 1848. At any rate, given a government of whim or caprice where land titles might be invalidated, customs levied, ports and trade routes closed, bribes demanded, immigration of friends and relatives prohibited, the right to bear arms circumscribed, imprisonment for no just cause carried out with no charges filed, and where constantly shifting political cabals dominated the national capital, it is remarkable that the settlers got along with the government as well as they did.

In 1827, when Hayden Edwards attempted a revolt against Mexico and proclaimed the Republic of Fredonia in east Texas, it was Austin and his followers who put down the revolt. Mexico, however, linked his activities to John Quincy Adams' efforts to purchase Texas, and a climate of suspicion was created. In 1828 and 1829 General Mier y Teran made an extensive inspection of Texas to determine what policy should be pursued toward the Texans, who now outnumbered the Mexicans in that province by about ten to one. His report caused alarm, asserting that the North Americans were taking over the country and would soon be powerful enough to make it independent of Mexico. He proposed that the government should (1) colonize Mexicans in Texas, (2) colonize Swiss and Germans, (3) encourage coastal trade between Texas and the rest of Mexico, and (4) place convict troops in Texas who would eventually become settlers. An 1829 proclamation forbidding slavery in Texas also became part of the plan to end the period of "salutary neglect" that Texans had enjoyed. In 1829, at the behest of Luis Aleman, a law was passed by the Mexican Congress that prohibited further colonization in Texas, established custom houses, and provided for garrisons of troops to be stationed at strategic points in Texas. The laws against slavery (however morally correct) and against further colonization, not only struck at the Texan's assumed customary right to property, they also made it difficult (if not impossible) for the *empresarios* to fulfill their contracts to bring in new families—threatening Texas with economic ruin. The proclamations of 1829–1830 were the most serious cause of friction between Mexico and Texas.

Direct confrontations between Texans and the Mexican government took place as a result of the implementation of the Mier y Teran plan. In 1831 the military posts at San Antonio, Goliad, and Nacogdoches were reinforced, and custom house forts were set up at Anahuac and at the mouths of the Brazos and Nueces rivers. A mercenary, Col. John Davis Bradburn, commandant of the garrison at Anahuac, in a moment of either arrogance or panic arrested Francisco Madero, a government land agent, and refused to accept his legitimate credentials. When William B. Travis and William Jack protested, they were also imprisoned in a brick kiln. When Jack's brother raised a sizeable force of the citizenry, Bradburn was forced to surrender his prisoner. By then the alarm was out, and a small force of Texans, bringing a cannon from Brazoria, fought a brief but bloody engagement with Mexican troops at Velasco.

Meanwhile, the "peace party" in Texas was attempting to dampen local enthusiasm for armed rebellion, and during the Bradburn affair they succeeded in persuading the people to adopt the "Turtle Bayou Resolution" which pledged loyalty and allegiance to General Santa Anna, who was at that moment conducting a successful coup d'état against the national government in Mexico. The Texans who adopted the Turtle Bayou Resolution were under the mistaken impression that Santa Anna was a liberal who would restore the Constitution of 1824 and with it the former loose federal structure of the Mexican government. The Bradburn incident passed, and the Texans were so overjoyed at Santa Anna's triumph that when he sent General Mexia north to chastise them, they greeted him warmly as an ally and overwhelmed him with "southern hospitality." Mexia, with no enemy to fight, returned to Mexico convinced that the Texans were loyal.

With their "ally" Santa Anna in power, the Texans decided that the time was auspicious for securing redress to their grievances stemming from the Mier y Teran plan, so in imitation of the American revolutionists they formed "Committees of Correspondence" to prepare a declaration of grievances to the Mexican government. On October 1, 1832, these committees sent delegates to a convention at Austin's capital at San Felipe de Austin. With Austin as president, they voted to demand that land titles in eastern Texas be guaranteed (this had been Madero's mission), additional *ayuntamientos* or local self-governing bodies be created there, customs duties be suspended for three years, prohibitions against immigration be repealed, and that Texas be separated from Coahuila and be made a separate self-governing province.

Since the immediate Mexican response to this convention was largely negative, a second convention was called in 1833—this time under the control of the "war party." This convention drafted a state constitution and dispatched Austin to Mexico City to present the Texan demands. In Mexico City Austin succeeded in persuading Santa Anna to accede to all the Texan demands except separate statehood, but not without a long and tedious struggle. Then, because of the discovery of an indiscreet letter which he had written in anger urging Texans to adopt separate statehood on their own, Austin was seized on his way home and thrown into prison for more than a year. Santa Anna was angry. He also appeared to be suffering from a Napoleon complex and desperate for absolute power. Nothing in the Mexican political tradition prevented him from repudiating his reform program, scrapping the entire federal system, dissolving the Congress and the state governments, which he did in April of 1834—proclaiming himself dictator of Mexico.

In 1835, when the dictator Santa Anna once again reestablished the military garrisons and custom houses in Texas, he merely added to the bitterness aroused by his imprisonment of Austin. And despite the fact that he had released Austin, Texans under Travis, a Byronic person who appears to have had a death wish, attacked the garrison at Anahuac, which quickly surrendered. Another engagement was fought at Gonzales. And an army of 500 men led by the now returned Stephen F. Austin routed the Bexar garrison and captured San Antonio. The latter was a remarkable house-to-house conflict in which the Texans battered their way through thick-walled adobe houses to ultimate victory. Still, true revolution had not taken place. After the conquest of San Antonio, the victors assembled in convention at San Felipe de Austin and paradoxically declared their loyalty to Mexico. Once again, following the American pattern, they submitted a "Declaration of Causes" similar to the "Declaration of Rights and Grievances" of 1775 designed to appeal to Mexican liberals. The Texans did not neglect, however, to install a local government and create an army with Sam Houston as its commander.

During this period of waiting, the public officials fell to quarreling; the army officers refused to cooperate; and Sam Houston took a leave of absence to look into Indian affairs in east Texas. When the provisional government met again, cooperation became somewhat more plausible, since news had reached the officials that Santa Anna was on his way with the flower of Mexican soldiery to crush their revolt. On March 2, 1836, they adopted a declaration of independence modeled on that of the American colonies and a constitution closely resembling that of the United States.

Despite their declaration, their constitution, and their resolution to cling together, the Texans found it difficult to weld an army out of individualistic frontiersmen. Because Col. Frank W. Johnson and James W. Fannin could not agree on a plan of united action, their small companies were destroyed piecemeal. Part of their force was destroyed near Refugio as it sought to help refugees fleeing eastward. The remainder of Fannin's command (some 350 men), largely volunteers from the United States, were surrounded and forced to surrender to the Mexican General Urrea at Coleto. Their surrender was unconditional, but no one expected the sequel.

They were marched to Goliad, where on Palm Sunday, 1836, they were taken out and shot, almost to the last man, under orders from Santa Anna.

The destruction of Fannin's force left Travis' command at San Antonio in dire circumstances. Including Davy Crockett's Tennessee volunteers, he had only about 155 men, half of whom acknowledged his leadership and the rest of whom preferred to follow James Bowie. Both Governor Henry Smith and General Houston had ordered Travis and Bowie to abandon San Antonio and retreat eastward to the main Texan encampment; Travis and Bowie had refused and, instead, moved to fortify the Alamo. Santa Anna and his army of 3000 men arrived at San Antonio on February 23 and then, for the Texans, retreat became impossible. After this, only James B. Bonham and 32 men from Gonzales entered the Alamo as reinforcements. The following day, Travis sent his famous letter from the beleaguered mission, "I am determined to sustain myself as long as possible and die like a soldier . . . *Victory or Death*."[5] By March 1, Santa Anna began launching all-out assaults, but the 187 Texans held firm. At last, however, on March 6, 1836, the main body of Mexican chivalry overwhelmed the Alamo defenders, killing Travis, Crockett, Bonham, and Bowie like ordinary mortals. No Texan defender except the wife of Almeron Dickinson survived, but Santa Anna had lost 1544 men killed and there were uncounted numbers of wounded. The Alamo defenders succeeded in delaying Santa Anna's mighty army long enough for Houston to assemble and equip a Texan force of about 900 men as he retreated hastily to the east. Thanks to the help of the old Missouri River steamboat, *Yellowstone*, he managed to cross the Brazos on April 12 and 13 and keep his force intact. Santa Anna, in pursuit, momentarily lost the fugitives and divided his army into three forces, each one being ordered to seek out and destroy Houston and his army. Then with the main Mexican force Santa Anna went into encampment at the juncture of Buffalo Bayou and the San Jacinto River just southeast of present-day Houston. His force numbered approximately 1200 men.

Meanwhile, Deaf Smith, a Texan scout, had captured the Mexican battle plans, which he gave to Houston. On April 21, with a

---

[5] Quoted from a facsimile of the Travis letter in the author's possession. The original is in the Texas State Archives, Austin, Texas.

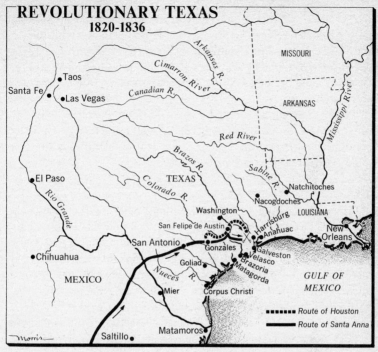

REVOLUTIONARY TEXAS
1820-1836

MISSOURI

Taos

Santa Fe

Las Vegas

Arkansas R.

Cimarron River

Canadian R.

ARKANSAS

Mississippi River

Red River

Brazos R.

El Paso

TEXAS

Colorado R.

Sabine R.

Natchitoches

Nacogdoches

Rio Grande

Washington

Harrisburg

LOUISIANA

San Felipe de Austin

Anahuac

Chihuahua

San Antonio

Gonzales

Galveston

New Orleans

Velasco

Goliad

Brazoria

Matagorda

MEXICO

Nueces R.

Mier

Corpus Christi

GULF OF
MEXICO

■■■■■■ Route of Houston
—— Route of Santa Anna

Saltillo

Matamoros

Morris

force of about 800 men, Houston attacked Santa Anna's encampment just at siesta time. While an improvised band played the romantic ballad, "Will You Come to the Bower I have Shaded for You," the Texan army charged across 200 yards of open field, no doubt remembering the Alamo and Goliad. Although they did not wreak such lethal destruction as the Alamo defenders, killing approximately 630 Mexicans, they succeeded in shattering the Mexican army. Revenge was total when later in the day Santa Anna was captured trying to escape as a common soldier. The appearance of Sam Houston, lying under a tree, his ankle having been shattered by a rifle ball as he led the Texan charge, was an interesting contrast to that of the Mexican dictator, who pleaded for his life in common soldier's garb.

Instead of executing Santa Anna as a war criminal, the Texans exercised uncharacteristic restraint. They gave him safe conduct via Galveston to the United States in exchange for his order to the rest of the Mexican forces to evacuate Texas. However, upon hearing the news of Santa Anna's defeat, the Mexican forces were already evacuating Texas with remarkable dispatch. In addition, to save his life, Santa Anna signed a secret agreement with the Texas provisional government acknowledging Texan independence. This was repudiated by the Mexican Senate as soon as Santa Anna was safely beyond the reach of the Texans; hence, technically, the war for Texan independence did not cease, at least from the Mexican point of view, until the Treaty of Guadalupe Hidalgo in 1848. During those intervening years a great deal of blood and treasure would be wasted to prove a point.

II

During all this civil strife and rebellion, what had been the attitude of the United States? Officially she was neutral, acknowledging treaties of amity and friendship to Mexico. Officially, too, the United States enforced its somewhat haphazard neutrality laws which prohibited recruitment of organized bands of men in the United States for the purpose of engaging in foreign wars. She contributed no American military personnel, not even "advisors," although in 1836, General E. P. Gaines crossed over into disputed territory near Nacogdoches to quell an incipient Indian uprising, incidentally freeing the Mexican garrison for other duties.

But, despite their country's official neutrality, American citizens greatly contributed to the Texan cause. Bands of men bound for Texas such as those led by Crockett, or "the New Orleans Grays," passed over the frontier as emigrants. In fact most of the men killed under Fannin at Goliad and many of the men in the Alamo and on the plains at San Jacinto were recently arrived Americans. The financing of the Texan army was the work largely of Stephen F. Austin, who borrowed his money in the United States. In addition, many private individuals contributed money, arms, and ships to the beleaguered Texans. Hence, as a people, the United States did not remain neutral. Given the Alamo and Goliad massacres, in which friends and relatives were lost, and in view of Santa Anna's essential lack of humanitarian and democratic qualities, United States support for the Texan cause can only be questioned by the most cynical of men.

Texan independence, once achieved, however, was ambiguous. For eleven months the United States withheld formal recognition of its independence, and President Jackson himself rejected an initial bid for annexation. His successor, Van Buren, did likewise. Hence Texas was forced to create and sustain an independent southwestern republic, which it did for eight years. It became another model of the Jeffersonian "sister republic."

III

But, although Texan overtures for annexation were rejected by two American presidents, the new republic to the Southwest was of vital interest to the United States, both in the realm of domestic politics and in foreign affairs. The primary reason for American refusal of the annexation proposals was the Texan stand on slavery. Mounting abolitionist sentiment in the United States, centering in New England, symbolized by William Lloyd Garrison's founding of *The Liberator* in 1833, and John Quincy Adams' abrupt reversal of his advocacy of Texan annexation over the question of slavery, made the passage of any annexation treaty virtually impossible and, for a president, politically disastrous. By 1837, President Van Buren, who was personally opposed to slavery, had enough trouble with the mounting financial panic of that year.

Aside from the personal moral convictions of American governmental officials, the more practical question of domestic balance of power overshadowed the Texan problem. If Texas were admitted to the Union, she might choose to divide herself into a number of smaller states which, when represented as slave states in the Senate, would give the South an overwhelming preponderance and hence bring the country to the brink of civil war. Thus for the time being, of necessity, Texas was forced to fend for itself.

In terms of American foreign policy, however, Texas represented a different kind of peril. In the event of another invasion of Texas by Mexico, southern and western public opinion might force the United States into a war with Mexico. On the other hand, Texan plans for expansion across the Southwest to the Pacific might ultimately block any American efforts in that direction and also bring on an armed conflict with Mexico to which the United States would undoubtedly be committed. Meanwhile Texas, politically disunited, virtually bankrupt, and in constant fear of Mexican aggression, provided an excellent target for British and French ambitions.

France, hostile to Mexico over the question of claims, recognized Texas in 1839. Britain held back because of the existence of slavery in Texas. Not until 1840, when Britain obtained a treaty stipulation calling for the abandonment of the African slave trade to Texas, did she grant full diplomatic recognition to Texas. Holland and Belgium followed suit.

Once having granted recognition to Texas, Britain began to display marked interest in Texan affairs. Guided chiefly by the Minister of Foreign Affairs, Lord Aberdeen, England had three important objectives with regard to Texas: (1) to bring about the abolition of slavery, (2) to bring Mexico to acknowledge the independence of Texas so that the new nation might serve as a check on the American advance to the Southwest, and (3) to establish favorable trade relations with Texas to create competition for southern cotton planters and to establish a market for English manufactured goods in Texas. Britain's position on slavery was one of morality and expediency. Having freed her own slaves in the West Indies and elsewhere out of moral conviction, she now used the abolitionist cause to prevent competition from cheap slave labor in other countries. Moreover, she hoped to use Texas cotton not only to provide competition for southern plan ers but to force the abandonment of protective tariffs in the United States. This would throw open the American market to cheap English manufactured goods produced by a system of mines and factories whose cruelly exploited white labor enabled England to undersell any country in the world on a free-trade basis.

To accomplish these aims, Lord Aberdeen devised several stratagems, and vacillated considerably in his tactics. Britain had to be the friend of both Texas and Mexico while encouraging each of them to pursue a policy distasteful to its citizens. In the case of Texas it was abolition. In the case of Mexico it was the abandonment of Texas. To accomplish these aims Lord Aberdeen was willing to take England to the brink of war with the United States, but not beyond. In 1843, when the threat of war arose, Aberdeen, after having formed an agreement with France to guarantee the territorial integrity of Texas against any foreign power—meaning the United States—hastily and with the help of the French minister Guizot abandoned the plan. Likewise he backed away from a plan to grant Britain the territory between the Nueces and the

Rio Grande rivers in exchange for aid to Mexico in its stand against Texas and the United States. Previously, in 1842, Aberdeen had been embarrassed by the Texan discovery of a British plan to supply Mexico with two armed steamships and British crews and, in the interests of diplomacy, he was forced to disavow this venture.[6]

In general, the British plan for Texas was to bring about its independence without bloodshed, and then to exploit it diplomatically and economically, vis-a-vis the United States. This was extremely difficult because of widespread sentiment for annexation in the United States and Texas, and because Santa Anna seemed disposed to use every British gesture of friendship as a signal to begin preparations for a renewed war of aggression against Texas.

Meanwhile, the Texan leaders waited for fortunate turns of events, pushed plans for internal development in Texas, and under Mirabeau Buonaparte Lamar engaged in disastrous attempts at expansion to the Pacific, exemplified by the ill-fated Texan Santa Fe Expedition of 1842, which lost its way on the Staked Plains and fell prey to the Mexicans. In resisting Texan efforts toward expansion and counterattack, Mexico did nothing to enhance her standing among civilized nations. The bedraggled members of the Santa Fe Expedition (mostly traders) were brutally treated and some were even murdered on their long terrible march as prisoners to Mexico City. In retaliation, Mexico invaded Texas twice in 1842, occupying San Antonio and holding some of its citizens as hostages. Texan belligerents, engaged in a retaliatory expedition against Mier, were captured and forced to draw lots (beans from a jar) to determine who would face the firing squad for trying to escape. A short time later a filibuster leader captured in Tampico was beheaded and his grisly remains triumphantly displayed in the public square for weeks as a demonstration of Santa Anna's power.

Diplomatically, the Texans played a more skillful game: they used Mexican atrocities and British interest to play on the emotions of American policymakers and public opinion. Conversely they used the threat of American annexation to spur England on in its efforts to persuade Mexico to acknowledge Texan independence.

The ascendency of Tyler to the presidency of the United States

[6] E. D. Adams, *British Interests*, pp. 79–96.

marked a turning point in the diplomatic struggle. Tyler favored annexation and worked for it. American public opinion was stirred by evidence that Britain had attempted to tamper with the internal affairs of Texas in the matter of slavery. In the face of Tyler's enthusiasm for Texas, the American furor over British abolitionist meddling, and the threat apparently posed by that country in general to American expansion, England was forced to walk softly and work for the election of Henry Clay, an anti-expansionist. She also abandoned neutrality with regard to Mexico and applied maximum pressure for the recognition of Texan independence until, by the end of 1844, England finally persuaded Mexico to grant a treaty of independence to Texas.

In the interim, Tyler's Secretary of State, Abel Upsher, who was skillfully piloting the annexation treaty through the Senate, was suddenly killed by the explosion of a naval gun aboard the cruiser, *Princeton*. John C. Calhoun, the new Secretary of State, took up the cause of annexation and, because he justified annexation on the grounds that more slave states would be a positive good, almost single-handedly caused the defeat of Tyler's treaty in the Senate. He antagonized the English by engaging in a debate over the antislavery correspondence of Richard Pakenham, the British minister, and he antagonized the abolitionists of the North and the moderates of the West such as Senator Thomas Hart Benton. The Senate rejected Tyler's treaty on June 8, 1844.

By this time, however, both the Whig and the Democratic conventions had met in Baltimore. The Whigs nominated Henry Clay, who, in a letter written from Raleigh, North Carolina, came out against annexation and expansion, while the Democrats nominated Andrew Jackson's protegé, James K. Polk, a dark-horse candidate from Tennessee who was a forthright expansionist. Polk shrewdly campaigned on a nationalistic platform calling for the reannexation of Texas and the reoccupation of Oregon. His more belligerent supporters, inspired by the taunts of political opponents, later adopted the slogan, "54° 40' or fight." In his desire for continental expansion, Polk showed no fear of Britain, and this put him in good favor with American voters.

Taking advantage of the political currents, Tyler changed his tack regarding the annexation treaty. He decided to submit it to Congress for acceptance by a joint resolution of both houses, where a simple majority rather than a two-thirds vote was needed for ratification. The strength of this maneuver was in the wording of the bill. The joint annexation bill made annexation subject to arrangements to be completed by the President. By this time Polk had been elected on what was taken to be a mandate for expansion and annexation, although he actually won over Clay because of a vote split in New York caused by James G. Birney's Liberty Party. Many of those who voted for annexation in February of 1845 did so because they believed that Polk would actually complete the arrangements. Even Benton stepped aside in his opposition, voting against his own bill. In an exchange on the floor of the Senate, Benton rose to succinct but admirable rhetorical heights.

Mr. Benton (from his seat): The Senator from Missouri will vote against it (laughter). . . . Mr. Miller said that the speech delivered by the honorable Senator had made a strong impression upon him, and he hoped the Senator would not destroy his own child.
Mr. Benton (from his seat): I'll kill it stone dead.
(General laughter, with an attempt at cheering, suppressed by the President).[7]

Tyler, however, signed the annexation treaty immediately on March 1, 1845, leaving the boundary arrangements to be completed by the new president. The annexation treaty was his and his alone. With this measure of satisfaction, he left office on March 4, 1845.

A short while later, on June 21, 1845, the Texan Senate voted unanimously to reject a last-minute Mexican treaty granting independence, secured through the efforts of Britain. In a curious historical circumstance, Andrew Jackson Donelson, the bearer of the American treaty, passed Captain Charles Elliott, the British bearer of the Mexican treaty, just outside of Galveston on the road to Austin.

Appropriately, on July 4, 1845, a special Texan convention assembled at Washington on the Brazos voted for annexation to the United States: on December 29, 1845, Texas was admitted to the Union. A long struggle seemed to be ended, but another and even greater series of conflicts was soon to begin.

---

[7] Quoted in William Nisbet Chambers, *Old Bullion Benton Senator From the New West* (Boston, Toronto: Little, Brown, and Company, 1956), p. 290.

CHAPTER III

"England, Beak, Talons and All"

I F JEFFERSON, Adams, Jackson, and Tyler had been ardent expansionists, willing to take great risks to extend the American continental empire, James K. Polk of Tennessee in this respect overshadowed them all. During his administration he made the eagle scream at its highest pitch. And yet, in March of 1845, as he stood on the portico of the capitol in a driving rain, his grizzled hair matted and swept back behind his ears, his grey eyes betraying little emotion as he took the oath of presidential office, he appeared to be an enigma. He was so in his own time and has remained such ever since.

"Who is James K. Polk?" his Whig opponents sneered in the election campaign of 1844. Who, indeed? He was a Democratic Party regular who had served seven terms in the House of Representatives, where he led the floor fight in Jackson's war on the Bank. He had been governor of Tennessee, leaving a safe seat in the House to campaign for the office out of a sense of party loyalty. At the time of his election to the Presidency, because he had refused a place in Tyler's cabinet, he was unemployed. But he was also the man who had seized upon the dramatic issue of the day, expansionism, and used it to defeat Henry Clay, the most-colorful if not the most-admired political figure of his time. Like Jackson, Polk had come out of the West to place himself at the head of the predominant popular enthusiasm—expansionism—and it had carried him as a dark-horse candidate to victory.

What were his plans for the presidency as he took office in March of 1845, facing a possible conflict with England in the far Northwest and certain war with Mexico over the annexation of Texas? His friend, Secretary of the Navy George Bancroft, remembered that at the beginning of his administration, slapping his thigh for emphasis, Polk declared, "There are four great measures which are to be the measures of my administration: one a reduction of the tariff; another, the independent treasury; a third, the settlement of the Oregon boundary question; and, lastly, the acquisition of California."[1] He carried out all of these objectives. And in retrospect, although historians have seen him as "Polk the Mendacious," a kind of stupid and stubborn Machiavelli, or "Polk the Mediocre," befriended by turns of good fortune and a capacity for hard unimaginative labor, one is somehow forced to agree with Bancroft, who wrote years later, that, even in his papers, "his [Polk's] character shines out . . . just exactly as the man he was, prudent, far-sighted, bold, excelling any Democrat of his day in undeviatingly correct exposition of his democratic principles; and in short, as I think judging of him as I knew him, and judging of him by the results of his administration, one of the very foremost of our public men, and one of the very best and most honest and most successful Presidents the country ever had."[2]

Bancroft, of course, was his friend; posterity has been left to wonder. Thanks to his lengthy but enigmatical diary that recorded deeds and policies rather than, as in the case of Adams, motives, introspections, and chains of reasoning, Polk has presented an inconsistent image to historians. At first, he was underestimated, and Whig historians, blaming him for shocking rudeness to England, cruelty to inoffensive Mexico, the extension of slavery, and the Civil War, conceded him nothing. After the work of Eugene McCormac, his major biographer, Polk's reputation began to grow, and the recent important work on his career, *Empire on the Pacific*, credits him with a master plan for the acquisition of California, the ports on the Pacific at San Francisco, Monterey, San Diego, and Puget Sound, so subtle and well conceived as to make him a virtual Talleyrand of world diplomacy.[3] Just as the earlier portraits concede him too little, recent interpretations perhaps read too much into his policy. This chapter and the next offer a somewhat

---

[1] Quoted in James K. Polk, *Polk, The Diary of a President, 1845–1849*, Allan Nevins, ed. (London, New York, Toronto: Longmans, Green and Co., 1929), p. xix.

[2] *Ibid.*, p. xviii.

[3] Graebner, *Empire on the Pacific*.

different assessment of him as he stood, the foremost brinksman of his time, facing the combined hostilities of England and Mexico.

I

As the new President, Polk had to deal with the questions of Texas and Oregon simultaneously, meanwhile keeping an eye on California. The Texas problem was the most immediate one since, upon the completion of annexation, the Mexican Minister Almonte called for his passports and left for home asserting that annexation was considered by Mexico as a virtual declaration of war.[4] Any dealings with Mexico were, however, intimately related to the question of Oregon and California since the latter formed the stakes, between England and the United States, of a war with Mexico.

American interest in the Pacific dated back to John Ledyard's landing on the Northwest coast with Captain Cook's expedition of 1776. Long before that, the Spanish, British, and Russians had been rivals for the coast dating back to Cabrillo (1542), Drake (1579), and Bering (1741). In 1790 the English in a show of force, had broken a Spanish monopoly of the Northwest coast trade by the Nootka Sound Convention. Americans first seriously contended for the Northwest with the voyages of the Boston ships *Columbia* and *Lady Washington*, which hunted sea otter off the coast in 1788-1789. In 1792 Captain Robert Grey, piloting the *Columbia*, discovered the Columbia River, although he did not officially claim it as United States territory. Following Grey, British vessels sailed up the Columbia River, which they had missed, like the Spaniards before them, in their earlier coastal explorations.

In 1793, the Canadian Sir Alexander Mackenzie completed his march across the continent through Canada to the Pacific, arriving at the Bella Coola River. He was followed by Simon Fraser who in 1808 with tremendous labor, maneuvered down the rocky river that bears his name. During this period, too, David Thompson crossed the Rockies and began exploring the upper Columbia and its tributaries deep into what is now Montana. Because of his concern for the fur trade, however, he spent his time building trading posts on the upper part of the river and its tributaries,

[4] George L. Rives, *The United States and Mexico 1821–1848* (New York: Charles Scribners Sons, 1913), Vol. I, pp. 589, 694.

and did not come down the Columbia until 1811 when, to his dismay, he found that the American agents of John Jacob Astor had already established a settlement at Astoria on the south bank of the river.

During and after the War of 1812 the Canadian Northwest Company traders held Fort Astoria and the Columbia country, although they could do little with it until the arrival of Donald McKenzie, a trader of great energy. McKenzie revived the fortunes of the Northwest Company in that quarter and made the Columbia outpost, once considered worthless, far more valuable. During the period when despondency prevailed on the Northwest coast, Britain and the United States had signed the joint occupation treaty of 1818. American claims to the area rested, of course, on the accidental discovery by Captain Grey, on the first settlement at Astoria, and on the daring march of Lewis and Clark in 1805. All of these American efforts occurred south of the Columbia, although Clark's actual claim was posted on a tall yellow pine overlooking Cape Disappointment on the north side of the river.

As British and American interest in the Northwest coast increased, the interest of Spain declined. By 1820 the sea otter trade was ruined by ruthless overkilling, and Spain retreated to the 42nd parallel in 1819, surrendering her rights in the Northwest to the United States. Upon the suddenly acquired Spanish rights rested the strongest American claim to land north of the Columbia River. Meanwhile, through the 1820's, interest in the Northwest coast was chiefly centered in the exploitation of the interior by means of the Columbia, and a trade in furs grew up on the ruins of the old sea otter trade to China. In this period, beginning in 1822, American vessels owned by Bryant and Sturgis of Boston also began trading for cattle hides along the coast of California. By 1829 Yankee traders from New England had a virtual monopoly of the California hide trade which was both legal and illegal, depending upon the whim of the current Mexican governor, as Richard Henry Dana's stirring narrative, *Two Years Before the Mast*, clearly indicates. Throughout the decades of the twenties and thirties the hide trade flourished until it reached a high point in 1838, when 200,000 hides from California were imported into Boston.

In addition to the coastal trade, Americans, coming from the

interior, began to enter California. In 1826 Jedediah Smith, a
Rocky Mountain fur trader out of St. Louis, was the first to
make his way across the Mojave Desert into California. There
he was befriended by various New England sea captains, as were
those who followed him in the 1820's—James and Sylvestre Pattie,
Richard Campbell, and Ewing Young. American sea peddlers from
New England had all the best of the coastal trade, but the Mexican government frowned on the intrusion of fur trappers from
the interior. Also during this period, the competition between
British and American fur traders which was raging in the vast
western interior along the Snake, the Green, and the upper Missouri, spread into California as Hudson's Bay brigades from
the north under Ogden, Laframboise, McLeod, and Work moved
south from Fort Vancouver on the Columbia into California as
far as San Francisco Bay. In 1829 Ogden crossed the Great Basin
and reached the Gulf of California. Then, in his return north-

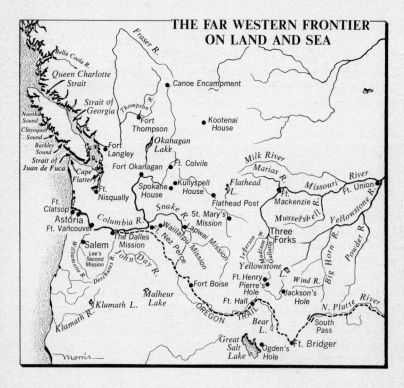

THE FAR WESTERN FRONTIER ON LAND AND SEA

ward to Oregon, traversed the entire length of Mexican California trapping as he went.

In the 1820's and '30's a great border of international rivalry
developed, encompassing the Pacific coast from San Diego to
Puget Sound, and stretching into the interior as far as the
headwaters of the Missouri. Much of the rivalry was on Mexican territory, but by the end of the 1820's that country was
virtually a helpless bystander as Britain and the United States
competed for western North America. No interpretation of American diplomacy for this period can afford to overlook the tremendous scope of this rivalry both on the coast and in the
interior. In terms of monetary value and the numbers of people involved, the rivalry for the coastal ports was greatest.
But the Hudson's Bay Company looked primarily to the interior, shipped its furs eastward over interior lines in Canada,
and was reluctant to concede a foot of prime beaver country
north of the Snake and west of the upper Missouri to the aggressive American fur traders. Likewise western politicians, the
most vocal supporters of Polk's belligerent Oregon policy, considered that their fortunes lay in the interior rather than on
the coast. By the 1830's they became more concerned with de-
veloping an internal commerce by means of settlement and the
outfitting of emigrants than with the "road to India." Senator
Benton spoke less about the Orient than about the fur trade
and settlement. His "fabled god Terminus," vanished forever to
be replaced by the boy hero Frémont, who in 1842 journeyed
west to the Wind River Mountains, raised a homemade eagle
flag on the highest peak, and called for the establishment of
forts and trading posts in the interior to aid the fur trade and
promote American settlement of that extensive region of mountains and river valleys. There were as yet few settlers in Oregon
and beyond the Rocky Mountains, but along the Mississippi
Valley lay the chief political strength for Polk's western policy.
Fortunately for the President-elect in 1844 this was reinforced
by the sentiment of some New England sea traders as well,
though in point of fact he made few inroads on the Whig voters
in that region in the 1844 campaign.

While Monterey and San Francisco were yearly becoming more
important focal points to Americans, Oregon too had great sig-

nificance, although not as a port on the Pacific since, until the advent of Charles Wilkes in 1841, few Americans had any familiarity with Puget Sound. However, in 1826 John Quincy Adams, ever mindful of New England's interests, had refused to bargain away American rights to that territory stemming from the Spanish treaty. In 1828 a treaty with Britain was signed which continued the joint occupation agreement indefinitely, specifying that upon one year's notice either party might terminate the agreement. This treaty worked greatly to American advantage, since in the late 1830's the type of people who moved into Oregon were settlers, while the British, oriented toward fur trapping rather than settling, gradually lost interest in the Snake and Columbia country, since they had deliberately stripped it bare of beaver to impede the advance of American fur traders. Under Governor Simpson's orders the main headquarters of the Hudson's Bay Company in the Northwest was moved northward in 1845 to Fort Victoria on Vancouver Island.

As the 1830's drew to a close, competition over Oregon and California became more intense. Eugene Du Flot de Mofras, a French explorer, came to admire San Francisco Bay and aroused mild French interest in that harbor. He also whetted British and American appetites. Captain Charles Wilkes returned from his expedition in 1841 and extolled Puget Sound and San Francisco Bay as the finest harbors in the world. Governor Simpson of the Hudson's Bay Company returned the courtesy in the same year and praised San Francisco. And as has been shown, since Andrew Jackson's offer to Mexico in 1835, there had been strong American interest in California north of the 37th parallel. Most of all, the three nations, England, France, and the United States, appeared to be worried that the entire coast, and with it the interior, would fall to one or the other power since it was so loosely held by Mexico. British agents in Mexico and the West were urgently advocating that the province be taken from Mexico as payment of outstanding claims. The British government, however, was engaged at the time in delicate relations with Mexico over Texas, and was disenchanted with the economic value of overseas colonies besides. The Foreign Office therefore sternly rebuked its Mexican agents. Instead the British government held fast to Oregon and pursued a policy of watchful waiting with regard to California, serving notice on Mexico that it would look with disfavor on the transfer of California to any other power. The United States felt the same way.

In 1842 Secretary of State Daniel Webster began to turn his attention to the West. Being a Whig from the trading state of Massachusetts, he proposed an agreement with Britain whereby the United States would relinquish to Britain the territory north of the Columbia and east of a line from the Admiralty Inlet on Puget Sound straight south to the Columbia if Britain would bring pressure on Mexico to sell to the United States all the land north of 35° north latitude—that is, territory including San Francisco. This was a shrewd and excellent trade as it related to ports on the Pacific, since it gave the United States Monterey, San Francisco, the Olympic Peninsula, and a harbor on Puget Sound, plus the mouth of the Columbia, assuming British success in pressuring Mexico into the cession. However, the strength of western sentiment for control of the interior was so strong that the House of Representatives refused to vote expenses for Webster's trip to England, and the plan collapsed.

By the end of Tyler's administration, both governments had expressed a wish to settle the Oregon question. The British wanted a Columbia River boundary. The Americans held out for an extension of the 49th parallel to the sea—an offer that they had repeatedly made to Britain without success.

By the time of the 1844 elections, however, the situation had changed. American settlers had begun to pour into Oregon. Frémont had sent dramatic dispatches from that country; mountain men and settlers had begun to form quasi-republican governments; and at least one trapper sent out a call for armed volunteers to "Sweep Oregon and California clear of the British."[5] Thomas Hart Benton arose in Congress to sound the call for "thirty or forty thousand American rifles beyond the Rocky Mountains that will be our effective negotiators" and which, presumably, would win Oregon for the United States.[6] British machinations with regard to Texas had stirred the West-

---

[5] Quoted in Charles L. Camp, ed., *James Clyman Frontiersman* Portland, Oregon: Champoeg Press, 1960), pp. 61–62.
[6] Thomas Hart Benton, *Thirty Years View* (New York: D. Appleton and Company, 1857), Vol. II, p. 482.

erners deeply. And finally, behind all of this, men of the North and West, seeing Texas about to become part of the United States, felt some need of just territorial compensation on their side of the slavery line to balance the Union. Such was the situation on the eve of Polk's campaign for the presidency.

II

Polk, of course, campaigned on the expansionist platform, or the "reannexation of Texas and the reoccupation of Oregon," although he never made clear what the latter phrase meant to him. Nor is it clear just exactly what his intentions were with regard to California. Certainly he wanted it, but the means he proposed to obtain it were not as yet apparent. One gets the distinct impression, behind the bland facade of his presidential diary, that he had no plan beyond "looking John Bull straight in the eye," and Mexico, too, if need be. Certainly he knew little of far Western geography, as his conversations with Frémont in 1845 attest. Upon his return from an extensive reconnaissance of Oregon and California in 1843–1844, Frémont was disappointed in his interview with Polk, who appeared to be proceeding on the assumption that a series of rivers flowed west across the Great Basin to the Pacific below the Columbia: "The President seemed for the moment skeptical about the exactness of my information and disposed to be conservative," Frémont remembered, "and not at all satisfied in his own mind that those three rivers were not running there as laid down [on the old maps]."[7] And in his lengthy presidential diary Polk mentioned Captain Wilkes only once. Clearly, though Polk showed some interest in Pacific ports, Wilkes' news about Puget Sound and San Francisco Bay was not uppermost in his mind. Nor was it in the mind of his Secretary of State, James Buchanan, who only mentions Wilkes twice in his own collected papers.

Rather, it must be concluded that Polk rode into the presidency on a general wave of enthusiasm for westward expansion with a marked antipathy to the British and Mexicans and, more important, a keen sense of domestic politics. Upon taking office, he set about securing the country's northwestern flank by dealing first

[7] Quoted in William H. Goetzmann, *Army Exploration in the American West, 1803–1863* (New Haven: Yale University Press, 1959), p. 103.

with the British in Oregon. Then he meant to take care of California and Mexico. This required him to retreat from the extreme 54°40′ position adopted by his most enthusiastic supporters. Using the excuse that he found himself embarrassed, if not committed, by the acts of his predecessors, he authorized Buchanan to offer a compromise at the 49th parallel giving Britain the rights to free ports south of that line on Vancouver Island. The British Ambassador, Richard Pakenham, dismissed this proposal out of hand, and at Polk's direction Buchanan withdrew the offer. Polk then grew belligerent. He invoked the Monroe Doctrine, served notice of the United States' intention to terminate the 1828 agreement, and adopted the stand of his western political backers— 54°40′ or fight. He did not, however, rush Benton's "thirty or forty thousand rifles" to Oregon, since at the same time he was facing a war with Mexico with a totally inept army at his disposal.

The Peel government and its Foreign Minister, Lord Aberdeen, however, inexplicably backed down at the crucial moment, just as they had done in the case of Texas. The trapped-out Columbia River was not worth a war, especially since the United States would undoubtedly have been able to defy the thirty ships of the line that Britain had at her disposal for an Oregon campaign by a retreat into the interior and a defense there in depth. Moreover, a war over Oregon might well have brought Mexico into the conflict as an unwanted ally and created the precise opportunity for an American subversion of California. Ultimately, too, British trading interests with the United States were far more lucrative and important than Oregon or trade with Mexico, especially since Polk was known to be an advocate of a free trade policy. Remote colonies, especially exhausted ones, were a burden. Free trade with a burgeoning, young power of the world was far more attractive.

Lord Aberdeen forthwith drafted an Oregon treaty that called for the 49th parallel as the boundary to the Strait of Juan de Fuca and provided guarantees for the property rights of the Puget Sound Agricultural Company on the Olympic Peninsula and the right of free navigation of the Columbia by the Hudson's Bay Company. When he received Aberdeen's treaty, Polk immediately submitted it to the Senate. Two days later, on June 12, 1846, the Senate voted for ratification. On June 15 Buchanan and Pakenham signed the treaty drafts, and on June 18 it was formally ratified by the Senate. No treaty ever had such an expeditious course through the legislative and executive branches of the United States government. Polk and his Congress had good reason for dispatch however, since the war of words with Mexico had escalated into armed hostilities.

In his Oregon diplomacy Polk had handled the affairs of the United States well. In a moment of great crisis, he had held firm and gained a treaty that was more than fair, considering the lack of any strong American claim, aside from that inherited from Spain, to land north of the Columbia.

In *Empire on the Pacific*, however, Professor Norman Graebner has interpreted Polk's actions with regard to Oregon from a somewhat different viewpoint, seeing the acquisition of the ports on the Pacific as the *sole* determinant of "the course of empire,"[8] and Polk as a single-minded schemer in this respect. Such a thesis requires re-examination. It depends upon several dubious premises: (1) the New England Whig merchant interests desired a port on the Pacific to the point of actual confrontation with Britain; (2) Webster in 1842 acted as their spokesman signifying their interest in the ports; and (3) Polk geared his far western policy according to their wishes.

To begin with, the New England Whig merchants were traders on a world horizon and had nothing to gain by the establishment of a political colony in the Northwest, particularly if it meant a direct confrontation with Britain. New England manufacturers were in competition with Britain and demanded tariff walls as a protection against foreign goods, but the shipping interests had their greatest market in Britain during this period, particularly since, by 1830, along with shippers from New York, they had gained control of the entire cotton export business from the South. Their ships loaded at southern ports, sailed northward to New York and Boston, then across the Atlantic to Britain. They returned the same way, eventually discharging cargoes of British goods on southern wharfs to the delight of affluent plantation owners. This formed the major bulk of northeastern trade, and a showdown with Britain over a remote port on the Northwest coast, or even over California, would have ruined this trade completely.

Second, it is by no means clear that Webster, although he may have fancied himself so, was the commissioned spokesman for

[8] Graebner, *Empire on the Pacific*.

New England interests in 1842 when he proposed his Northwest boundary commission to England. In the Northeast Boundary Treaty he had recently bargained away legitimate New England territorial rights to his friend Lord Ashburton, a representative of the house of Baring, and because of his connection with Tyler's Southern cabinet he was hardly regarded as a loyal New Englander in his home state of Massachusetts. In fact, by 1842 he was in serious political difficulties in New England. Given his aspirations for the presidency, he was in the position of having to cast about for some means of political redemption, one which would, if possible, remove him from his untenable position in the Tyler cabinet and get him out of the country. The Northwest boundary project became his means of redemption and escape.[9] But the sentiment for this maneuver was amply demonstrated by the refusal of the House to vote funds for his mission to the Court of St. James. One can only conclude that there was little interest in his project.

Finally, the most important question is: How much attention did Polk pay to the Whigs in shaping his expansionist objectives? They had opposed his campaign for the presidency; they had opposed expansion of any kind; they had opposed rupture of relations with Britain, and they stood squarely against any belligerent policy with respect to Mexico. Thus the thesis that Polk's policy was essentially Whig-inspired and geared solely to the acquisition of Puget Sound must be emphatically rejected. A western man, Polk had a dim view of maritime interests. His knowledge of Oregon geography was almost nil, and was limited to the Columbia River and to trade in furs. His hostility to the Whig Party was marked. The urgency of a solution to the Oregon question was paramount, in view of Mexican hostility. Therefore it appears that Polk simply worked to push the Northwest frontier as far as he could to gain control of the Columbia and thus satisfy his western constituents; and his estimate of how far the frontier had to be pushed to gain this objective was the 49th parallel. The most that one could grant the Whig-inspiration thesis is that the Senate, moved by Whig persuasion, which is dubious, forced Polk to accept the boundary treaty with Britain. Even this does not demonstrate that Polk had any far-reaching port-on-the-northwest-Pacific objective. Rather it suggests the converse.

[9] I am indebted to Mr. Robert Dalzell of Yale University, who called this fact to my attention when I sought his advice on Webster's political role in Massachusetts.

A more likely pressure on Polk was that of the seaboard South represented by Calhoun and McDuffie who wished no war with Britain over Oregon. In order to avoid such a war, this faction repeatedly insisted on compromise at the 49th parallel, which it was felt, Britain would accept. Even the expansionist fur trade representative Benton was willing ultimately to settle for this, given the alternative of war.

From first to last, Polk was a western man. Vast stretches of territory to the west, southwest and northwest with the potential for settlement and internal commerce had a simple appeal to him. Oregon and even California were primarily internal and continental projects. Therefore one must conclude that Polk was a courageous, even stubborn, diplomatic bargainer, but that he was no master, nor even a serious student of the currents of world maritime trade and the subtle geopolitics related to it. Rather he was moved by a variety of motives, of which the acquisition of a port at Puget Sound was the least important.

A consideration of the Texas and Oregon questions, however, reveals something of the "grand strategy" employed by Britain in competition with the emergent United States in this period. Since the Revolution, her strategy with regard to the United States had been twofold: (1) containment and (2) fierce economic competition on the high seas, in the fisheries, in the northern and northwest fur trade, and by dumping into this country cheap manufactured goods which wrecked the infant American industries after the War of 1812. As America grew, despite all odds, she became a prosperous nation, and hence a profitable market, particularly in the South, but also in the North and West in spite of tariff barriers. Therefore any policy directed toward the United States had to be subtle and tempered with caution. Given the ever-present menace of distresses in Europe, the American market became increasingly important.[10] However, this consideration had to be

---

[10] Polk's advocacy of a low, or "free trade" tariff in his first annual message to Congress had important diplomatic repercussions. It commanded the attention of British businessmen and it generated a spirit of caution in Britain with regard to Oregon. The London Economist asserted that an American free trade policy would justify British surrender of Oregon. Polk's "brinksmanship" was therefore also tempered by economic incentives to Britain. See James P. Shenton, Robert John Walker: A Politician from Jackson to Lincoln (New York and London: Columbia University Press, 1961), pp. 76–77.

weighed against the astonishing rate of American growth and expansion across North America and on the high seas, with the accompanying belligerence that was so characteristic of a newly emergent nation. At some point, therefore, the strategy of containment had to be employed, gently but firmly in the same way that this strategy had been employed in Canada, in the Northeast, in the Northwest, in California, in the Caribbean, in the Far East, on the high seas, and in Texas. Aberdeen and the British government clearly wanted no war that would disrupt American trade (the work of Prof. Ephraim D. Adams adequately demonstrates this), but wherever she could Britain did attempt, without marked success, to contain the rising American empire.

A second strategy also came into play after 1830. This was a variation on the old themes of divide and conquer, and balance of power. Here the British abolitionist movement provided an unexpected weapon. As serious controversy over slavery began to develop in the United States after 1821, the possibility of an American civil war appeared, particularly with the headlong rush of Americans into the vast spaces of the West. In its vigorous, worldwide campaign against slavery, the British movement gave strength to American abolitionism—indeed, it lionized the disunionist William Lloyd Garrison at the world antislavery convention in England, and the movement even won over that staunch old unionist John Quincy Adams, to the point where he opposed the annexation of Texas, an area he had previously coveted.

By the 1840's, because of the work of the abolitionists and the dispute over slavery, Lord Aberdeen confidently expected an American civil war.[11] Given the unofficial leverage of the world antislavery movement, Britain's official policy could be one of watchful

---

[11] Adams, *British Interests*, p. 221 and footnote. This is an especially important passage and deserves quotation in full, since Adams did not see fit to include a transcript of any of Aberdeen's numerous statements on this subject. It reads: "The constant object of that diplomacy was to maintain peace on the North American continent. He believed that British interests were secured only by such means, and that, while Great Britain need fear no United States aggression upon Canada, the steady expansion of the United States portended no good; and he again predicted, as a result of expansion, civil war in the United States which might or would involve British interests also. This was not Aberdeen's first prophecy of civil war in America, but it is, perhaps, the first time that he made it an excuse for British policy."

waiting, and perhaps gentle pressure on Texas to mend its im-
moral ways. Every note advising Texas to abolish slavery, however, only called attention to its existence and intensified the
American division over slavery. Significantly, nothing was said
about peonage in Mexico and the Latin American republics. In
fact, Texas and the American South were the only major economically developed parts of the globe where slavery officially existed,
and therefore any "world" abolition campaign perforce was directed primarily at the United States. During the Texas crisis re-
sponsible British foreign ministers and ambassadors repeatedly
"leaked" their private resentments against slavery while officially
disavowing any intent to tamper with a nation's internal institu-
tions.[12] These "leaks" of unofficial sentiment served two purposes.
They helped cement an alliance between northeastern American
Conscience Whigs and Britain, and they continually elicited in-
dignant protestations from spokesmen for the American South.
The most notable example of this was the clumsy ranting of John
C. Calhoun who, in response to English goading, placed the Texan
annexation treaty on the none-too-lofty grounds of slavery and
southern states' rights. Here British strategy worked perfectly.
The distasteful Pakenham correspondence relating to abolition in
Texas was politely disavowed, but Tyler lost his treaty because of
heightened tension over slavery. Only adroit maneuvering on the
part of the President reversed a lost cause and gained Texas for
the United States.

The possible effects of the British strategy regarding slavery
were diverse. If expansionist sentiment of all types could be stifled
as the result of the furor over Texas and slavery, the United States
could be contained—in the Southwest, in California, and in the
Northwest. If Texas could be made to remain independent and
abolish its slavery, it would serve as a competitor to the South and
as a docile, noncompetitive market for British goods. But these
by 1844 were remote possibilities. A more promising result would
be the division of the Union, probably between North and South,
but also, given this, among North, South, and West. The West,
through its ports on the Gulf of Mexico and its Mississippi artery,
would become an enormous market for British trade. The South
would revert to the status of a British economic protectorate,

---

[12] *Ibid.*, pp. 141–165.

since its cotton crop and its slaves were already mortgaged to English bankers—particularly the house of Baring. Slavery could be officially, although not practically, abolished and the whole southern economy reconstituted to suit British needs. Also the extravagant plantation way of life was ideally suited for the marketing of British goods. Finally, without its internal markets in the South and West, the North with its close cultural and economic ties to England might turn back to the mother country, or at least take on a status similar to that of Canada.

Even if none of these regions surrendered its sovereignty, the continuous rivalry between them would create an ideal balance-of-power situation in North America, and Britain's most serious potential world rival would be checked. It did not take open belligerency to bring this about, however. It could come about only by gentle persuasion, official forthrightness, and the enflamed passions of romantic and emotional men in North America. Historians may never know, perhaps, the extent to which this grand view of world strategy was consciously and fully developed in the minds of English policymakers, but reflection upon their deeds and both official and unofficial statements reveals its outline with remarkable clarity. Perhaps only the victory of Union troops at Gettysburg in July of 1863 prevented the ultimate fulfillment of the British grand design.

In view of all this, the signing of the Oregon treaty in the summer of 1846 seems almost anticlimactic. For, by the time the treaty was signed, war had begun with Mexico and the United States had taken the final step on the road to a continental empire that could mean triumph or catastrophe.

CHAPTER IV

"War . . . by the Act of Mexico"

A MERICANS ACCUSTOMED TO reflecting on their internal history often consider the Civil War as the most important event in mid-nineteenth-century American history. Not so to the many Latin Americans who in the mid-twentieth century are assuming an increasing importance in world affairs. If one were to graph the significant events in mid-nineteenth-century American history from the Latin American point of view, none would assume larger significance than "the War of the American Intervention" in Mexico. The rise of the United States to the rank of a major world power, coupled with the subsequent retardation of Latin American development, has made the United States campaign in Mexico seem one of unbridled aggression—a monstrously unequal contest between the "colossus of the North" and weak, inoffensive Mexico.

At the outset of the war, however, the contest was not nearly so unequal, nor was the United States so completely assured of victory as current slogans and historical hindsight have made it seem. Prior to the outbreak of hostilities, the United States had an army of less than ten-thousand men led by senior officers who had never commanded so much as a full regiment in the field. Its fleet, scattered around the world, lay at the mercy of possible British intervention. The government in Washington had almost no knowledge of the Mexican terrain of rugged mountains and vast rocky plateaus over which an invading army would have to fight. In addition, there were the disadvantages of a 2000-mile supply line, the seasonal fevers, and the wild country that favored Mexican defense and guerilla warfare. Only the naiveté of a youthful country and its leaders would have sought such a war. Be that as it may, the war came, and a sound reassessment of it is perhaps more important now than at any time in our history.

I

Most serious American histories of the Mexican War are clouded by the overtones of guilt and moral justification implanted by several generations of Whig and neo-Whig historians who somehow, and quite falsely, have connected its campaigns with the question of slavery and the "aggressive slavocracy." With the exception of the work of Justin Smith, the most thorough to date, the majority of American histories of the war have been Whig-inspired apologetics indicating little concern for world strategy and a disregard for the actual facts of the coming of the war.[1]

Concerning this disregard for the facts, it is clear that war was declared both officially and unofficially by Mexico on at least two occasions, and in a third instance when she could have prevented war, Mexico refused to do so in a most offensive and belligerent manner. In 1845, when the Texan annexation treaty was being consummated, Almonte, the Mexican minister to the United States, delivered an ultimatum to the American government. On behalf of his government he served notice that Mexico would "consider equivalent to a declaration of war against the Mexican Republic the passage of an act for the incorporation of Texas with the territory of the United States; the certainty of the fact being sufficient for the immediate proclamation of war."[2] He could have stated his country's intentions in no plainer language; and the intent of his government was made even clearer when, hearing of the passage of the annexation treaty, Almonte requested his passports and left for Mexico. In Mexico, the American ambassador was dismissed and sent home.

Later, on April 23, 1846, President Paredes of Mexico officially declared a "defensive war."[3] During the interim, Mexico refused

---

[1] See, for examples, Peter T. Harstad and Richard W. Resh, "The Causes of the Mexican War, A Note on Changing Interpretations," *Arizona and the West*, **VI** 289–302 (1964).

[2] Quoted in Justin Smith, *The War with Mexico* (New York: The Macmillan Co., 1919), Vol. I, p. 84.

[3] Bemis, *Diplomatic History*, p. 241.

all American overtures for peaceful adjudication of the differences between the two countries—instead she began mobilizing an army and proclaiming the invincibility of Mexican arms. Indeed she repeatedly declared her intention of reconquering Texas.

The United States, on the other hand, could not really afford a war at the time of the British crisis over the northeastern and northwestern boundaries. For one thing, the outbreak of war might make California a hostage to Britain and result in the occupation of that territory by elements of the British fleet. So concerned was the United States over California, the hostage, that in 1842, fearing British occupation of that territory, Commodore Thomas Ap Catesby Jones, a none-too-intelligent commander of the American Pacific Squadron, rushed northward from Peru and seized Monterey. Discovering his mistake, he lowered the United States flag, saluted that of Mexico, held a fiesta, and sailed away. The United States, like Britain, was not prepared to take California forcibly from Mexico. It would purchase it, if possible; it would not take it. However, it would not stand by while the Pacific province fell into foreign hands. California was in truth a hostage for the good behavior of both Britain and the United States, although Mexico failed to recognize it as such, or even to recognize its value as a place ready for economic development.

American policy with regard to Mexico in 1845 had, therefore, to be a delicate one designed to achieve its aims, short of war. What were American aims in 1845? They were (1) a peaceful adjustment of the Texas boundary, (2) the securing of American claims against Mexico going back to its revolution in 1821, and (3) the acquisition, by purchase, of all or as much as could be acquired of the country north of a line running west from El Paso to the Pacific, including the rich trading mart at Santa Fe, and California together with the major Pacific ports from San Diego northward.

The first two of these objectives were reasonable. The latter was presumptuous, but clearly in the interests of the United States, interests which the President had once sworn to uphold. The Texan boundary was not of such vital importance to the United States as to warrant a war, although it called for some brinkmanship characteristic of the day. It could have been settled short of war by conceding the territory to the Nueces, despite the fact that a Texan *empresario* had settled people in that country prior to the war for Texan independence.[4] The matter of claims was different. In the nineteenth century the government was sworn to uphold the just claims of its citizens abroad, and at least $2 million in claims against Mexico had been confirmed by outside adjudicators. For a long time Mexico refused even to consider them, and then when she did, acknowledging their validity, she defaulted on payment of interest in 1843. She could, however, raise money for war against Texas, for the purchase of steam warships from Britain, for the construction of palaces and cathedrals adorned with burnished gold, and she could afford gorgeous plumage and extensive haciendas for her leader, General Santa Anna. She could also afford the widespread graft and corruption of her rapidly shifting public officialdom and her numerous provincial armies. Under these circumstances American importunateness was perhaps justifiable. Certainly the United States was not more importunate than the British or the French, whose warships blockaded the Mexican coast and whose troops invaded Mexican soil over the question of the claims. Therefore, only the impetuous American offer to purchase her northern provinces could have given Mexico just cause for indignation.

But this is, of course, logical speculation, and the situation in Mexico was anything but logical. It was a divided country in grave internal turmoil; federalists, republicans, rich landholders, monarchists, the Church, and the military were all powerful contending factions, and out in the provinces virtual war lords maintained whatever government there was. In 1845 Santa Anna, the man who had once united Mexico, was in Cuban exile, and his means of uniting Mexico were strictly limited to rousing a militant anti-Americanism. The President of the Mexican Republic was J. J. de Herrera, whose administration was threatened daily by the military faction under Mariano Paredes. No Mexican leader who aspired to permanency in office or, beyond that, to the stabilizing of his country could afford to be "soft" on Americanism. Hence the United States became the victim of Mexican internal political strife. Given the irrationality of the situation, the most pacific policy might well have been to abandon the question of the Texan

[4] Rupert Richardson, *Texas, The Lone Star State* (Englewood Cliffs, N. J.: Prentice Hall, Inc., rev. ed., 1964), pp. 57–58.

border to Mexican caprice, leave the claimants to shift for themselves, and pursue a policy of watchful waiting with respect to California, especially since revolution in that province was certain to come eventually. But Polk was a president who was ambitious rather than mendacious—above all dedicated to his sworn duty; and he pursued a different course.

II

Polk's policy was calculated to settle peacefully the differences between the two countries, but to the maximum advantage of the United States. Accordingly, he exhausted all possible means of diplomatic negotiations; at the same time, threatened by open Mexican hostility and preparations for war, Polk mobilized United States military resources on land and sea. This would enable him to bargain from strength at the conference table. It would also prevent Texas and California from falling into Mexican and British hands if a military crisis came. Serious mobilization began in Mexico in the early summer of 1845. The United States followed suit shortly thereafter.

In June 1845, Secretary of the Navy George Bancroft issued orders to Commodore Sloat, commanding the Pacific Squadron, to hold himself in readiness to seize California if a war should break out, but in the meantime to commit no belligerent act. On July 25, the President, after evidence of Mexican preparations for war, ordered General Zachary Taylor with an army of 4,000 men to occupy a position on the edge of the disputed territory. General Taylor chose Corpus Christi at the mouth of the Nueces River. His troops had orders to refrain from engaging in any hostile action against Mexico.

So concerned was Polk with preventing a possible outbreak that when he learned that Senator Benton had dispatched his son-in-law, Captain John C. Frémont, to California at the head of a band of tough mountain men armed with a military howitzer, he immediately sent a messenger to stop the expedition. The messenger was too late, and Frémont proceeded on his way contrary to orders.

There has been dispute among historians as to whether Frémont went out to California on the orders of Benton or Polk. Frémont himself claimed to have secret orders from Secretary of the Navy George Bancroft, and when war came, he was, to be sure, apprised of it by Lt. Archibald Gillespie of the United States Marines, who had originally been sent with messages from Polk to Consul Thomas Larkin. However, some historians question the existence of any secret instructions, and they regard Frémont merely as Benton's meddlesome agent in California.[5] Benton claimed "credit" for Frémont's activities in the Bear Flag Revolt of 1846, and his story is corroborated by the fact that the Pathfinder had indeed been sent on a different mission in the vicinity of Santa Fe by his commanding officer in the Corps of Topographical Engineers, Colonel J. J. Abert.[6] Polk, therefore, appears to have had very little to do with Frémont's adventure, although the Pathfinder's operations in California were in line with Polk's later instructions to Consul Thomas Larkin in October of 1845. At that time Larkin was advised to be ready to subvert California in the event of war.

With his military preparations already under way, Polk turned to negotiation. He publicly, although not privately, ignored Mexican belligerency, and on the ship that took Almonte back to Mexico, he dispatched a "confidential agent," William S. Parrott, whose mission was to sound out the Herrera government to see if it would agree to accept a "minister" empowered to discuss the crucial issues between the two countries. In Mexico Parrott proceeded to follow instructions and, through the United States Consul John Black, he received encouragement from the Mexican Foreign Minister, Manuel Peña y Peña. In a dispatch of August 16, 1845, Parrott wrote, "The President [Herrera], who thus far has received the unanimous vote of the Departments for the high office, is known to be in favor of an amicable arrangement of the effervescenses pending with us, and has been heard say that if a minister from the United States should arrive he would be well received; of this, however, I will be better informed before the departure of the British Express about the last of the present month."[7]

Moreover, Black, on October 15, 1845, managed to obtain a written statement from the Mexican Foreign Minister stating that President Herrera was "disposed to receive the commissioner of

---

[5] See especially George Tays, "Frémont Had No Secret Instructions," *Pacific Historical Review*, **IX** 151–171 (1940), and John A. Hussey, "The Origins of the Gillespie Mission," *California Historical Society Quarterly*, **XIX** 43–58 (1940).
[6] See William H. Goetzmann, *Army Exploration in the American West*, pp. 116–117.
[7] Quoted in Bemis, *Diplomatic History*, p. 235 footnote.

the United States, who may come to this capital with full powers from his government to settle the present dispute in a peaceable, reasonable, and honorable manner."[8]

Mexico also quite rightly demanded that an American naval squadron in the vicinity of Vera Cruz be ordered away before Mexico would receive a minister. Parrott brought this information back to the United States with him in November, 1845. As soon as he received it, Polk commissioned John Slidell of Louisiana, a not altogether happy choice in view of the late Texas unpleasantness, as "minister plenipotentiary" empowered to negotiate with Mexico upon all outstanding matters. Polk's instructions to Slidell were (1) to assume all American claims if Mexico would concede the border at the Rio Grande, (2) to try to buy, though not as a sine qua non of the Texas border negotiations, all of Mexico's northern provinces from the El Paso line northward and across to the Pacific for $25 million, although Polk was prepared to go higher, and (3) failing this, to offer $5 million for New Mexico. This third commission, incidentally, reveals that Polk was as much interested in the interior trade with Santa Fe, the object of anxious clamor by his western constituents, as he was in the California ports.

With instructions in hand, Slidell departed from Pensacola, Florida, for Mexico. Unfortunately, by the time he reached Mexico, the Herrera government, in dire jeopardy, refused to receive him, using as an excuse that it had not agreed to receive a "minister plenipotentiary," which signified renewed diplomatic relations between the two countries, but only a "minister" to negotiate the Texas boundary difficulties. The Paredes government, which soon overthrew Herrera, fearful of public opinion (meaning that of the chief power factions in Mexico City) also took this position. It was, of course, a pointed insult to the United States, and a foolhardy refusal of a chance to avert war and save the northern provinces. Instead, Mexico continued its mobilization for war.

When Slidell reported the complete failure of his mission on January 12, 1846, Polk immediately ordered General Taylor and his army to move from Corpus Christi to the Rio Grande opposite Matamoros. There he took up a defensive, but vigilant, position of joint occupancy with his Mexican counterpart, General Arista. Taylor did not seize the Nueces-Rio Grande country: he

[8] Quoted in Julius W. Pratt, *A History of United States Foreign Policy*, 2nd ed., (Englewood Cliffs, New Jersey: Prentice-Hall, Inc., 1965), p. 128.

simply stationed his troops there. The Mexican army was free to do the same since the status of that territory had not yet been determined.[9]

Finally, on May 9, Polk called a meeting of his Cabinet and proposed sending a war message to Congress regarding the question of the claims. He had exhausted his patience with Mexico and, although a war involved greater military risk than he suspected, Polk intended to fight to obtain not only the claims but also all of the coveted territory. The Cabinet was behind him, except Bancroft, who wisely demurred, fearing the intervention of the British fleet. The meeting had adjourned with Polk ready to submit his war message the following day, when news arrived from the Rio Grande that Mexican cavalry had attacked Captain Thornton's command, killing and wounding several American soldiers and taking the rest prisoners. Later General Arista boasted, "I had the pleasure of being the first to start the war."[10] This incident had occurred on the north bank of the Rio Grande, but it did not matter to Polk in any case. He hastily reconvened the Cabinet on the evening of May 9, and the members unanimously approved the war message he presented to Congress two days later declaring, "War exists by the act of Mexico herself." On May 13 Congress affirmed that, "by the act of the Republic of Mexico, a state of war exists between that Government and the United States." By that time General Taylor with 2,000 troops had already won the battles of Palo Alto and Resaca de la Palma on the American side of the Rio Grande, and the Mexican army of 6,000 demoralized men was in full retreat. When the victorious American soldiers examined the personal baggage left behind by Arista after Resaca de la Palma, they found an order from the Mexican Government directing him to "forward" Taylor to Mexico City as a prisoner.[11]

III

The field campaigns of the Mexican War form one of the most remarkable chapters in American military and cultural history. Flung out over thousands of miles of difficult terrain, these cam-

---

[9] Smith, *The War with Mexico*, Vol. I, pp. 148, 154.
[10] Quoted in Smith, *The War with Mexico*, Vol. I, p. 155.
[11] Otis A. Singletary, *The Mexican War* (Chicago: University of Chicago Press, 1960), p. 32.

paigns accurately reflect the innocence and naïveté of the romantic American to whom nothing was impossible, and no risk too great. Marching in ragged bands over mountains and deserts, confronting the unknown at every hand, the Americans were both conquerors and explorers, and the result of their efforts was continental America.

With the declaration of war, Congress authorized the raising of 50,000 volunteer troops while Polk and General Winfield Scott settled down to plan the strategy of attack on Mexico. Although the American campaigns were intended to be offensive rather than defensive, their objective was not the actual destruction per se of the Mexican army. Rather each of the armies sent into the field had a strategic political and territorial objective. Taylor's army was to stabilize the situation on the Rio Grande, and march south to capture Monterrey; then it would be in a position to hold all of northeastern Mexico. An auxiliary force under General Wool was ordered south via Taylor's route. Its objective was the capture of Chihuahua, the main economic center of north-central Mexico. Col. Stephen Watts Kearny with "the Army of the West," which included a large number of mountain men and St. Louis traders as volunteers, was to head for Santa Fe and, having conquered it, Kearny was to march overland and aid in the seizure of California. A supplementary force of volunteers would march south from Santa Fe to El Paso and assist General Wool in the capture of Chihuahua.

Meanwhile the navy had orders to converge on California, seize it from the Mexicans, and hold it against possible British or French intervention. In the Gulf of Mexico the first naval objective was the capture of Tampico and the blockade of Mexican ports. All of these maneuvers on land and sea were designed to hold the northern provinces of Mexico rather than to assault the seat of government itself. Polk and his generals believed that once these objectives were attained, Mexico would cease fighting, concede the required territory, and sue for peace. However, in June of 1846 Polk made a serious mistake. In the belief that by restoring the exiled Santa Anna to power, he could bring the war to a speedy, negotiated end, Polk ordered an American force to convoy the Mexican leader to Vera Cruz, and allowed him to assume control once again in Mexico. Santa Anna was venal and cruel, but he loved glory and, once back in power in Mexico, he took up the fight against the Americans. He pursued it so vigorously that what had been planned originally as a war of provincial conquest soon required a march on the Mexican capital and the subjugation of all Mexico before peace could be attained. General Scott undertook this task himself by landing at Vera Cruz and marching over the mountains to Mexico City.

The conception of a grand strategy and its execution are not precisely the same thing. Taylor's victories at Palo Alto and Resaca de la Palma—and the capture of Matamoros—had been relatively easy. But when he began to march his army southward toward Monterrey, difficulties arose. Despite the fact that he had Henry King's small river steamboat to transport his troops upstream to Reynosa and Camargo, the problems of logistics and discipline were formidable. Volunteers engaged in brawls with regular soldiers who were acting "superior." Atrocities were committed on civilians, and guerilla attacks made life more hazardous than expected. Even the place that Taylor chose for his grand encampment, Camargo, proved to be bad. It was a breeding ground for yellow fever, and the soldiers called it "dreadful Camargo." One man described it as "a yawning graveyard."[12]

Eventually, however, Taylor assembled his forces and marched them 200 miles across the dry plateau of north Mexico to Monterrey. There, in a furious four-day battle from September 20 to 24, he defeated the forces of General Pedro Ampudia, and after an armistice period, took possession of the city. Because of Taylor's poor leadership, however, the Americans lost 500 men in the fight. Employing the main army to hold the Mexican garrison behind its strong fortifications at the eastern end of the city, Taylor sent General William Jenkins Worth on a flanking attack around the western end of the city where, in a furious assault, he captured the Bishop's Palace and the heights overlooking the town. From this point, the American artillery could be effective. However, instead of merely holding at the strongly fortified eastern end of the city, Taylor ordered a series of assaults by the Third and Fourth Infantry Regiments. The assaults proved to be disastrous as Mexican lancers cut down the charging infantrymen, and Mexican gunners firing from two strong forts subjected Taylor's men to a

[12] *Ibid.*, p. 34.

murderous fire. Although the ultimate capture of the city required house-to-house street fighting, the major American casualties were in Taylor's unnecessary assaults on the strongest Mexican fortifications.

After an honorable surrender was arranged and General Ampudia marched off to the south beyond Saltillo, Polk ordered Taylor to occupy Saltillo but to go no farther. Taylor, however, suspicious that Polk wished to rob him of his glory (and possibly the presidency), moved south of Saltillo to La Angostura, a narrow pass commanding the road to San Luis Potosi. At this point General Scott came to Saltillo and took many of Taylor's best troops in preparation for the campaign against Vera Cruz. Therefore, despite reinforcements received from Wool, Taylor's army on the rocky plateaus of Buena Vista numbered only 4,700 men.

Santa Anna, having intercepted a dispatch from Taylor and Scott, knew of Scott's proposed assault on Vera Cruz—also of the weakened condition of Taylor's army. Assembling a marvelously caparisoned force of 20,000 troops led by his best generals— graduates of French military schools—Santa Anna led his army north to attack Taylor's men. The battle of Buena Vista, perhaps the most valorous feat of American arms in the entire war, took place on February 23, 1846, on the hard lava plains just north of La Angostura. Taylor's small army was strung out across the main road, his artillery and breastworks situated on the long fringes of high ground coming down from the mountains to his left. His guns commanded the only road. To the right of the road was a series of massive, eroded gullies that made an attack from that direction impossible.

When Santa Anna appeared, he offered Taylor the customary terms of surrender which Taylor, his palmetto hat and white duster shielding him from the sun, impolitely declined. Then Santa Anna, after ordering his assembled and glittering soldiers to celebrate high mass with incense and trumpet music, attacked. His main assault was well conceived as he sent his cavalry around to the base of the mountains at Taylor's left, shattering his flank and severing the road to Saltillo at the rear of his army. On the first assault the battle was nearly lost as the Indiana regiments crumpled before the Mexican advance. But, just in time, Taylor came up with a regiment of the red-shirted Mississippi Rifles led by

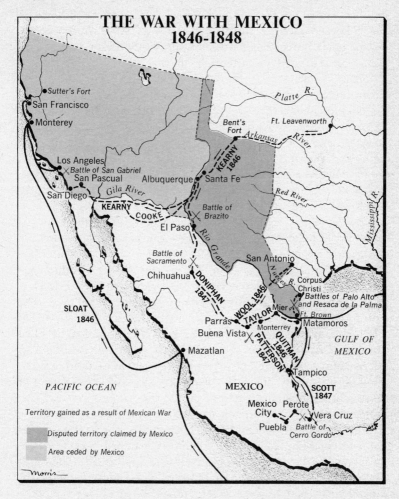

THE WAR WITH MEXICO
1846-1848

Sutter's Fort
San Francisco
Monterey

Platte R.

Bent's Fort
Ft. Leavenworth

Arkansas River

Los Angeles
Battle of San Gabriel
San Pascual
Albuquerque
Santa Fe
San Diego
KEARNY 1846

Gila River

Red River

KEARNY
COOKE
Battle of Brazito

El Paso

Rio Grande

Mississippi R.

Battle of Sacramento
Chihuahua
San Antonio

DONIPHAN 1847

Nueces R.
Corpus Christi
Battles of Palo Alto and Resaca de la Palma

SLOAT 1846

WOOL 1846
TAYLOR

Mier
Ft. Brown
Matamoros

Parras
Buena Vista
Monterrey
QUITMAN 1846

Mazatlan

PATTERSON 1847

GULF OF MEXICO

PACIFIC OCEAN

MEXICO

Tampico

SCOTT 1847

Mexico City
Perote
Puebla
Battle of Cerro Gordo
Vera Cruz

Territory gained as a result of Mexican War

Disputed territory claimed by Mexico

Area ceded by Mexico

Morris

Jefferson Davis and, in a gaudy, bloodcurdling charge, they drove
the Mexicans back and secured the flank. That afternoon Santa
Anna attacked again, but his men were cut down by the mobile
artillery brought into play by Braxton Bragg and other future
Civil War leaders. After one more assault on the center of the
American lines, Santa Anna retired—his army shattered. That
night behind a camouflage of campfires he led his battered army
southward toward San Luis Potosi. Taylor's men awoke, expecting

another attack, but they found themselves masters of the field in the greatest American victory of the war. After Buena Vista, Taylor made no further moves toward the Mexican capital, but rather concentrated his attention on that other capital—on the Potomac.

Meanwhile to the north, in New Mexico, because of the adroit diplomatic maneuverings of Senator Benton, Kearny had conquered Santa Fe without firing a shot. Benton had sent the trader James Magoffin ahead of Kearny's army to conduct secret negotiations with the New Mexican Governor, Armijo, and Magoffin had succeeded, possibly for a significant sum of money, in persuading Armijo not to defend New Mexico.[13] So the Governor fled southward uttering threats while Kearny occupied Santa Fe.

From Santa Fe a column of volunteer troops led by the Missouri lawyer Alexander Doniphan marched south across the dreaded *Jornada del Muerto* (approximately at present day Los Alamos) to El Paso. There in the battle of Bracito the American volunteers slaughtered a force of brave Mexican attackers on Christmas Day, 1846. From El Paso the intrepid Doniphan marched his men, later called "Doniphan's Thousand," deep into Mexico all the way to Chihuahua where they met and, through sheer bravery, defeated General Garcia Condé's vastly superior force in the battle of Sacramento. Doniphan now found himself 500 miles deep in Mexico with no supply line and a major city to hold. But instead of staying at Chihuahua, where he would ultimately have been defeated by guerillas, Doniphan marched his men across Mexico to Saltillo and joined General Wool. Then finally, their terms of enlistment expiring, Doniphan's volunteers marched back to Matamoros where they were loaded on ships and returned to New Orleans as heroes. The march of "Doniphan's Thousand" was the longest single march in American military history.

While Doniphan and his men were covering themselves with glory, the Army of the West was faring badly. Kearny, at the head of 300 dragoons, headed west along the Gila for California. On the lower Rio Grande he met Kit Carson, who told him of the successful conquest of California. Kearny sent half of his men

[13] Susan Shelby Magoffin, *Down the Santa Fe Trail and into Mexico*, Stella Drumm, ed., foreword by H. R. Lamar (New Haven: Yale University Press, 1962), pp. 84, 264–265.

back to Santa Fe and headed out across the Southwest with a much reduced force, guided by Carson. This was the first official American exploration of the far Southwest, and out of it came Lt. William H. Emory's important scientific report and map—a map which guided thousands of emigrants over the Gila Trail to California in 1849.

However, when Kearny's small force arrived in California, instead of finding a subdued territory, it met a belligerent force of Mexican lancers at San Pascual on the road to San Diego. In a classic cavalry charge Kearny and his men clashed with the lancers and suffered defeat. Kearny lost one-third of his men while the Mexicans lost three lancers. The battle ended several days later when the Americans, barricaded at Snooks Ranch but ready to fight to the last, were rescued by a detachment of sailors and marines brought by Kit Carson from San Diego.

While Kearny was moving west, the conquest of California, which in view of the fears of British intervention should have gone most smoothly, was badly bungled. Commodore Robert F. Stockton and Captain Frémont worked at cross purposes, allowing the Mexicans to recapture most of southern California. Not until two pitched battles were fought under the direction of the wounded Kearny at San Gabriel and the Plains of Mesa did California actually fall to the United States. In the interim, in New Mexico a revolt by the Indians of Taos had succeeded to the extent of massacring and horribly mutilating Governor Charles Bent and some of his officials before General Sterling Price's troops put down the uprising. The conquest and the maintenance of a continental empire were not proving to be as easy as expected.

The final campaign of the war was one conducted by General Winfield Scott. On March 9, 1847, he succeeded in landing at Vera Cruz and within a few days had reduced and captured the supposedly impregnable castle of San Juan de Ulloa. Then he marched inland over the national road to Jalapa. On the road to Jalapa, Scott and his men fought a fierce encounter at Cerro Gordo. There Santa Anna, who had fled southward after Buena Vista, had assembled another formidable army which chose to stand at the narrow pass of Cerro Gordo. Because of a daring piece of reconnoitering by Captain Robert E. Lee, Scott knew of the Mexican defensive positions. In a two-pronged assault, directly into heavy enemy fire Scott's men captured the heights above Cerro Gordo and also the artillery positions commanding the road. One veteran of Monterrey wrote home, "The fight at Cerro Gordo was, while it lasted, the fiercest one I was ever in."[14] (He died a few months later at the gates of Mexico City.)

At Pueblo, General Scott paused to regroup his army, which was daily facing disaster from the constant attacks of guerillas and bandits on his exposed supply line.[15] Like Doniphan and Taylor, he was far into Mexico, but in this densely populated part of the country, he was in daily fear of partisan uprisings. For ten weeks in the summer of 1847 Scott remained at Pueblo recruiting his men and attempting by means of an armistice to come to peace terms with Santa Anna. The Mexican leader meanwhile was busily engaged in quelling the peace party in Mexico City and raising another army to defend the capital. Ultimately, Scott was forced to cut himself off completely from his base of supplies, march seventy-five miles into the Valley of Mexico, and take the capital. The capture of Mexico City—another remarkable feat— was accomplished in a series of battles now famous—Contreras, Churubusco, Molino del Rey, Chapultepec Heights, and finally the assaults over the two causeways from Chapultepec to the twin gates of Mexico City. When General Scott and his army entered Mexico City they had conquered one of the largest capitals in the world. Even in the hour of victory it was by no means certain that they could hold the city—but they did. With the conquest of Mexico City the shooting war with Mexico, on all its vast fronts, was over.

IV

If, in general, it may be said that "the United States always wins the war and loses the peace," this was not true in the war with Mexico. But the winning of peace with Mexico involved a sequence of daring, of intrigue, and perhaps of accident that was

---

[14] Private Barna Upton to Elias Upton, Jalapa, Mexico, May 16, 1847 MS., Yale Historical Manuscripts Coll.

[15] For an insight into the difficulties with Mexican guerillas, see *The American Star*, an occupation newspaper published by the Army. Also see Emmett T. Hughes, *Rebellious Ranger Rip Ford and the Old Southwest* (Norman, Okla.: University of Oklahoma Press, 1964), pp. 22–56.

unparalleled in American diplomatic annals. It took place in two distinct stages. As the Whig General, Taylor, moved on to glory and prominence, and General Scott seemed destined to follow with more of the same, President Polk's political instincts came to the fore, and he began to search for a way to end the war to American advantage before the Whig generals could fight their way to the White House. In November of 1847 a curious and unique opportunity presented itself. Moses Yale Beach, the editor of the expansionist *New York Sun*, arrived in Washington and called on Secretary of State Buchanan, offering his services to help end the war with Mexico. It appears that Beach had been approached by Mirabeau B. Lamar and James Cazeneau of Texas, who in turn had been approached by the Mexican General Almonte with a plan for peace that had been sanctioned by a number of prominent Mexican politicians, particularly by high-ranking members of the clergy. This plan involved three points: (1) the occupation of California by the United States and all territory north of 26°, with responsibility for defense against all Indian raids into Mexican territory to be assumed by the United States; (2) the payment by the United States of its citizens' claims against Mexico, and the payment of an additional three million dollars as compensation for all territory thus occupied; (3) the restoration in good order to Mexico of the fortifications and public buildings and property taken during the war, and the refraining from any levies or forced loans upon the Mexican people.[16]

Beach himself had important business interests in Mexico which included a plan to create a new national bank of Mexico and an attempt to gain a franchise for a land route across Mexico's Isthmus of Tehuantepec. Since he was a well-known banker to Latin American nations, and had good connections in Mexico, Beach's offer to serve as a secret American peace agent had every prospect of success. On November 21, 1846, Buchanan made him "Confidential Agent to the Republic of Mexico."[17]

A short while later Beach sailed from New York with his daughter and a lady not his wife. The lady was Jane Storms, the greatest and perhaps the only female filibuster. Born Jane

---

[16] M. S. Beach, "A Secret Mission to Mexico," *Scribner's Monthly* XVIII, 136 (May, 1879).

[17] *Ibid.*, p. 137.

McManus in 1807, the daughter of a New York politician and friend of William L. Marcy, Jane McManus had married William Storms; along with her brother she had sailed for Texas in 1832. She first gained notoriety when in 1833 she was named corespondent in Madame Jumel's divorce suit against Aaron Burr, who was then seventy-seven years old. Testimony introduced in court alleged that a servant girl had seen Jane McManus and the aged Burr in some highly indelicate behavior, and on one occasion upon accidentally entering Burr's chamber Jane McManus was heard by the servant girl to utter, "Oh la! Mercy save us!" to cover her embarrassment.

By 1833 however, Jane McManus was in Texas, and it appears that she agreed to serve as corespondent in order to attain a new start out in the Mexican province. During her years in Texas she had come to know Lamar, Cazeneau, and other Texas figures. Indeed, she eventually married Cazeneau and went to live in a sod house near Eagle Pass while intriguing in the 1850's to detach the northern provinces from Mexico. By the time she accompanied Beach on his mission she had become a newspaperwoman for the *Sun*, a militant Texan expansionist, and under the name of Cora Montgomery, the authoress of a number of articles about the Southwest. She was to prove very valuable to Beach.[18]

The confidential agent and his entourage sailed for Cuba in December of 1846 and then, traveling under British passports, they went to Vera Cruz and into Mexico. In Mexico they made contact with the various factions that formed the peace party and commenced the drafting of a treaty. On April 14, 1847, Polk mentioned a letter from Beach in Mexico:

It is clearly inferred from his letter that he will make a treaty with them [the peace faction] if he can. Should he do so and it is a good one, I will waive his authority to make it, and submit it to the Senate for ratification. It will be a good joke if he will assume the authority and take the whole country by surprise and make a treaty. Mr. Buchanan's strong impression is that he may do so.[19]

The peace faction's move depended upon Scott's conquering Vera Cruz, and so as soon as Scott landed, Beach dispatched his assistant

---

[18] The best sketch of Jane McManus (nee Storms, nee Cazeneau) is in Edward S. Wallace, *Destiny and Glory* (New York: Coward-McCann Inc., 1957), pp. 245–275.
[19] Polk, *Diary*, pp. 217–218.

Jane Storms through the Mexican lines to Scott's beachhead with the details of the peace plot. Unfortunately Scott did not believe her since, because of his upbringing, he did not comprehend such a thing as a female agent, and he went about his military duties as usual.[20] Jane, it appears, made herself comfortable in the military camp and, it was rumored, became the mistress of Franklin Pierce.

Meanwhile, Beach, his efforts temporarily thwarted by Santa Anna's sudden return to power after the disgrace at Buena Vista, worked mightily to arouse the clergy against the Napoleon of the West, and in so doing he created a financial crisis for Santa Anna, since the clergy withheld the money that he needed to supply his new army; an uprising by Gomez Farias, inspired by Beach, pinned down the men that Santa Anna needed to oppose Scott at Vera Cruz. Eventually, however, Santa Anna prevailed, and also discovered Beach's role. Beach, warned by the American Consul, Black, fled to Tampico, his peace mission a failure just when it was on the verge of success. His work and that of Jane Storms remain one of the great and little-known stories of the secret diplomacy of the Mexican War.

In April, 1847, Polk commissioned another and more successful peace agent, Nicholas P. Trist, chief clerk of the State Department. Trist, who was a friend of Beach, had once as a young man been Thomas Jefferson's law clerk, and he was an old-line Democrat of minor standing. If Trist could make a treaty with Mexico then the credit would go to Polk and the Democratic Party. The inflated reputations of the Whig generals would collapse. Trist's instructions were to obtain a boundary running up the Rio Grande to the point where it intersected the southern boundary of New Mexico, the whole of the provinces of New Mexico and Upper and Lower California, and the stipulation that the United States should have the right of passage across the Isthmus of Tehuantepec. In return, the United States would pay Mexico up to $30 million, or up to $25 million if the isthmian passage were not secured, or up to $20 million if Lower California were not included. At the Cabinet meeting Robert J. Walker, Secretary of the Treasury, expressed his opinion that the Tehuantepec passage rights were more important than New Mexico and the Californias.

---

[20] M. S. Beach, "A Secret Mission to Mexico," p. 139.

Trist thus departed for Scott's army in Mexico to arrange a treaty. When he arrived at Scott's camp, he refused to show the general his sealed instructions from Buchanan and ill will developed between the two men that was dispelled when Scott gave Trist, of all things—a jar of guava jelly! After that peace offering they became friends, much to the annoyance of Polk. With Scott poised before Mexico City, the General and the agent procured an armistice with Santa Anna with a view to getting the Mexican leader to sign the treaty, which he seemed prepared to do. Once again Mexican nationalists rose up, however, and this time deposed Santa Anna, who fled Mexico while Scott occupied the capital.

Polk, now furious with Scott and Trist for granting the armistice (and, probably, over Scott's glory at conquering the Halls of Montezuma), recalled Trist and prepared to send Buchanan to do the negotiating. But Trist, seizing his own moment of glory, happily enough in the interests of peace, determined to remain in Mexico and negotiate his treaty anyhow, which he did at the little town of Guadalupe Hidalgo on February 2, 1848. Trist's treaty, deplored by Polk, actually rescued the United States from a precarious situation, which his partner General Scott knew only too well. If the treaty had not been consummated at that time, one more Mexican government would have collapsed, and the war might have continued indefinitely. In that case, Scott's position, deep in Mexico, would have become untenable. Possible British intervention might have resulted and, in the long run, the United States might have lost the war as well as the peace. Trist, a strange eccentric man who stood firm against political pressures back in the United States had won the peace. He was one of the few hero-diplomats in American history.

Trist's treaty secured the required Rio Grande boundary, the line across to the Pacific, and thus the entire northern provinces including Arizona, New Mexico, California, Utah, and Nevada. He did not secure the right of transit across Tehuantepec or Lower California, and in future years his lack of precision in defining the southern boundary of New Mexico necessitated the Gadsden Purchase. Nevertheless he had done well. He had acquired all of this territory for a grand total of $8.5 million, and he had extricated the United States from a costly war that its President had never wanted. This did not save Trist, however, who was immediately removed by Polk.

Nevertheless the President sent Trist's treaty to the Senate, which ratified it on March 10, 1848. The Mexican War was ended, and with it the intrigue, the jealousy, the militancy, and the "deeds of glory way out yonder under the setting sun."

Under Polk the nation had faced its gravest crisis since the War of 1812 as it confronted both Great Britain and Mexico and thus the possibility of two wars at the same time. But out of the crisis had come a continental empire stretching from the Atlantic to the Pacific, including golden California. The Mexican menace was forever quieted, and the British put on the defensive in Canada. But with the acquisition of the extensive new territory came the perils of maintaining it, especially California, and the ultimate peril of disunion. In the years to come the United States faced a mounting series of ever graver crises in the Caribbean, across the wide Pacific, and most of all at home as section fought section for control of the new territories while our former vanquished adversaries waited for the nation to fall to pieces.

For Polk, however, the time of crisis was nearly over. Exhausted by his four years of strain in the White House, where each year he had grown visibly more feeble, Polk died on June 15, 1849, a few months after leaving office. For him the price of security had come very high, but despite the odds and the opposition and vilification he had paid it, and well.

CHAPTER V

"Of Mountains and Mosquitoes
and Fever'd Tropic Isles"

T HE ACQUISITION of an American continental empire as a
result of the successful prosecution of the Mexican War
brought with it not only internal political dissension, but an official concern for the ultimate protection, security, and development of that empire. In 1848, shortly after the ratification of the
Treaty of Guadalupe Hidalgo, the discovery of gold in California
was announced and that remote province became more precious
than ever. As Americans saw it, the security of California and the
newly acquired Southwest depended upon three things: (1) the
acquisition and development of a secure communication route
across the United States or Central America to the Pacific Coast,
(2) the acquisition of Cuba, which would bring with it control
of the Caribbean and the approaches to a Central American communication route, and (3) the prevention of British or French
control of any or all of these strategic locations. Although the war
was over, and California, the hostage, had been delivered into
American hands, still there was fear throughout the country that
Britain, by closing the Caribbean to Americans and asserting its
existing control of the high seas, would render California as useless as it had been under Mexico—forcing California and parts of
the West to break off from the Union in their own best interests.
And, as will be seen, Britain's strategy in the Caribbean gave
good cause for alarm throughout the decades of the forties and
fifties.

Beyond the question of security, however, as an impetus to
expansion into the Caribbean and Central America there was the
vision and promise of economic opportunity—a virulent romantic
fever that had seized Americans of mid-century and would not

74

be quelled. James D. B. DeBow, the New Orleans editor, put it in its most comprehensive form in 1850:

We have a destiny to perform, a 'manifest destiny' over all Mexico, over South America, over the West Indies and Canada. The Sandwich Islands are necessary to our eastern, as the isles of the Gulf to our western commerce. The gates of the Chinese empire must be thrown down by the men from the Sacramento and the Oregon, and the haughty Japanese tramplers upon the cross be enlightened in the doctrines of republicanism and the ballot box. The eagle of the republic shall poise itself over the field of Waterloo, after tracing its flight among the gorges of the Himalaya or the Ural mountains, and a successor of Washington ascend the chair of universal empire! . . . The people stand ready to hail tomorrow . . . a collision with the proudest and mightiest empire on earth.[1]

The times therefore produced an expansive temper, "an age," as one writer has put it, "when few Americans cared what the rest of the world thought of them—what they thought of the rest of the world was all that mattered."[2] Along with those who were earnestly and seriously concerned for American security and union went another breed of men: venal seekers after colonial and exploitative wealth who masqueraded as patriots and Americans to conceal their true role as latter-day Conquistadores. The story of Central American diplomacy in the 1840's and 1850's is as much their story as it is that of the well-intentioned, but sometimes less efficient, diplomats.

I

Before the Mexican War was finally ended, President Polk had turned his attention to the Caribbean. In his instructions to Trist regarding the treaty he had urged the acquisition of a right of transit across Tehuantepec to facilitate passage to California. In addition, on December 12, 1846, an obscure American diplomat, Benjamin A. Bidlack, had negotiated a treaty with New Grenada (Colombia) that guaranteed to the United States and its citizens "the right of way or transit across the Isthmus of Panama upon any modes of communication that now exist, or that may hereafter be constructed." Tolls charged for such transit should be no higher than those charged the citizens of New Grenada. More-

[1] Quoted in Van Alstyne, The Rising American Empire, p. 152.
[2] Wallace, Destiny and Glory, p. 302.

over, the United States agreed to guarantee the "perfect neutrality of the before-mentioned isthmus," and "the rights of sovereignty and of property which New Grenada has and possesses over the said territory."[3] This, of course, was the important first step in securing an isthmian transit route, and it began the long process that culminated in the present Panama Canal.

Polk's continued interest in Central America was sustained by agents from Yucatan who spread rumors of a British attempt to take over that province. So moved was he that in his message to Congress on April 29, 1848, he invoked the dormant Monroe Doctrine as a warning to the European powers to refrain from intervention in that part of the world, and requested authorization to send United States soldiers to the peninsula. Even as he was speaking, however, bands of American volunteers returning from Mexico were heading for the exotic Mayan province as filibusters and mercenaries. Their expedition, the first of many such sorties in Central America, was an ill-fated one. They found no British, but the native revolutionaries—masters of jungle warfare—were more than a match for raw courage and the headlong charge customarily employed by American veterans of the Mexican War.[4]

However much he was alarmed by the rumors from Yucatan, Polk's primary interest was in Cuba. This interest was sustained, as Richard Van Alstyne has pointed out, by John L. O'Sullivan (who had family ties in Cuba), Moses Yale Beach (the constant intriguer), Robert Campbell (the American Consul-General in Havana), Stephen A. Douglas, Jefferson Davis, and the agents of the United States Mail Steamship Company and its Havana subsidiary, Drake Brothers.[5] On May 10, 1848, Polk recorded a visit from O'Sullivan and Douglas in his diary, describing their efforts to interest him in the purchase of Cuba. He concluded, "Though I expressed no opinion to them I am decidedly in favor of purchasing Cuba and making it one of the States of the Union."[6] Accordingly he commissioned Buchanan to draw up instructions to Romulus M. Saunders, the American Minister in Madrid, that authorized him to offer up to $100 million for

---

[3] Bemis, *Diplomatic History*, pp. 245–246.
[4] Wallace, *Destiny and Glory*, pp. 31–52.
[5] Van Alstyne, *The Rising American Empire*, p. 150.
[6] Polk, *Diary*, p. 321.

Cuba. In his instructions to Saunders, Buchanan stressed the danger to American trade of possible British acquisition of the island. He wrote: "Of what vast importance would it, then, be to her to obtain possession of an island from which she could at any time destroy a very large portion of our foreign and coasting trade."[7]

However, American concern with Cuba was not solely due to fear of Britain. In fact there existed a surprising unanimity of interest in the island throughout the United States. Southerners, such as Jefferson Davis and Robert Campbell, wanted it as a new state to expand slave territory within the Union. O'Sullivan and Moses Yale Beach, besides being instinctive expansionists, had investments in Cuba, as did the United States Mail Steamship Line and its New York backers. Stephen Douglas saw it as a market for products from the upper Midwest which would travel over his Illinois Central Railroad. American interest in the island covered a surprisingly comprehensive range of public and private concern in all regions of the country.

Unfortunately, however, Spain refused to sell. Queen Isabella II was hard pressed for cash, but Cuba was the remaining jewel of a disintegrating Spanish Empire. And she remained faithful to it although it cost her dearly. She steadfastly resisted the pressures brought by August Belmont upon her creditors (the house of Rothschild), the fiery blandishments, and intimidation of the Louisianan Pierre Soulé and the non-too-subtle threats emerging from the Ostend meeting of Buchanan, Soulé, and Mason in 1854.

Buchanan was distraught. "Above all we must not suffer its transfer to Great Britain," he declared, "We shall acquire it by a *coup d'état* at some propitious moment. . . ."[8] In the years 1849-1851 this very opportunity seemed to have arrived, and the filibuster Narciso Lopez sailed off from New York and New Orleans on three separate occasions with bands of men recruited in the United States to "liberate" the island. Port authorities either were intimidated by the armed red-shirted ruffians or officially classified them as "emigrants" bound for California via the Isthmus. Lopez proved to be a wretched general, however, and the Cuban people did not, as expected, rise to his aid. As a result, he was

[7] Van Alstyne, *The Rising American Empire*, p. 151.
[8] Van Alstyne, *The Rising American Empire*, p. 151.

defeated and ultimately captured. He and most of his men were executed: Lopez, in the peculiar Spanish way reserved for traitors—by the garrote, an iron collar placed around the neck and tightened by means of screws until strangulation resulted. Lopez was said to have taken it calmly seated in a chair. But this was not the case with one of his American comrades who, so the possibly apocryphal story goes, when given the chance to write a last letter home before execution seized upon a desperate stratagem. He would write to Daniel Webster, the Secretary of State, whom he had never met, in hopes that the Spanish would be wary of executing a friend of the exalted Daniel. He wrote:

Dan, my dear old boy, how little you thought when we parted at the close of that last agreeable visit of a week, which I paid you the other day, that within a month I should be 'cribbed, cabined, and confined' in the infernal hole of a dungeon from which I indite this. I wish you would send the Spanish minister a case of that very old Madiera of yours, which he professes to prefer to the wines of his own country, and tell him the silly scrape I have got myself into, if indeed it be not too late, for they talk of sending me 'to the bourne' tomorrow. However, one can never believe a word these rascals say, so I write this in hope that they are lying as usual—and am, my dear old schoolmate, your affectionate friend.[9]

Miraculously he was saved from the firing squad.

The fate of the Lopez expedition made other filibusters wary, however, and while Soulé was importuning Isabella to sell Cuba and threatening her with the hollow rhetoric of the Ostend Manifesto, General Quitman of Mississippi spent years getting ready for another invasion. However, by the time he was ready, in the mid-fifties, he was a tired old soldier and was easily persuaded at the last minute not to make the attempt. Thus, despite all the frantic American efforts, Cuba continued to hang like a slightly overripe kumquat in the tropical Caribbean until the end of the century. Even Britain did not dare pluck the forbidden fruit.

II

While Cuba remained a coy temptress for Americans to the end, better success was achieved on the Isthmus, although the seduction necessitated a long series of lover's quarrels, with Britain as usual the rival and corespondent. As far back as the buc-

---

[9] Quoted in Wallace, *Destiny and Glory*, pp. 99–100.

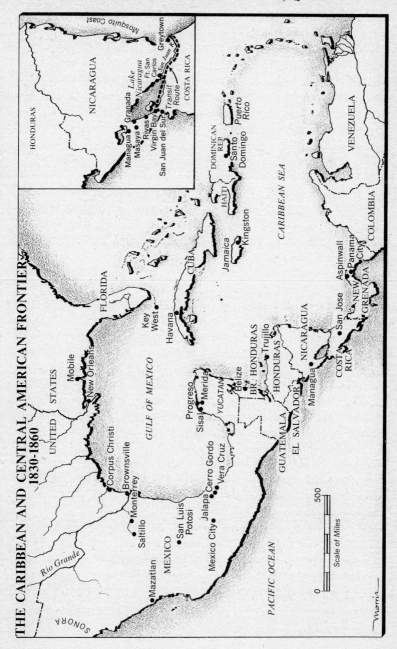

THE CARIBBEAN AND CENTRAL AMERICAN FRONTIER 1830-1860

caneer days of the sixteenth and seventeenth centuries, England had maintained a certain interest in Central America and, gradually through the years, she managed to establish a colony at Belize (now British Honduras). Despite the fact that in several treaties she had ceded Belize, in 1840 an agent in residency was sent to that territory and it was proclaimed a crown colony. The next year, growing increasingly mindful of the importance of the Caribbean as a hedge against American expansionism, Britain seized the Bay Islands, which dominated any possible Guatemalan or Honduran transportation route. According to Samuel Flagg Bemis, "The history of Belize is a fine example of how successful buccaneering can lead to territorial encroachments, to settlements, to sphere of influence, to a protectorate with expanding boundaries, and to actual sovereignty."[10] Belize and the Bay Islands form a model of subsequent British and American activities in Central America.

Looking outward from the Bay Islands, Britain suddenly discovered what she considered an "injustice" on the Nicaraguan coast: another, and perhaps the best, canal route. Accordingly in 1844 while the United States was watching California, a British representative was sent to Bluefield (on the Nicaraguan Coast) to look into the effect of this injustice on the Mosquito Coast Indians. By 1848 the Mosquito Coast had been proclaimed a British protectorate. The ancient town of San Juan, strategically overlooking the entrance to any Nicaraguan transit route, was occupied by "Mosquitan" forces under British guidance, and was renamed Greytown, no doubt because of the shadowy nature of its birth. Nicaragua quite naturally appealed to the United States for help, and President Polk sent the Kentuckian Elijah Hise to that country to see if any further injustices had been done. By 1849 Hise managed to sign a treaty with Nicaragua which granted the United States exclusive rights of transit, including the right to fortify the route and a guarantee of the territorial integrity of Nicaragua. Another remote but significant world boundary signifying international rivalry had suddenly appeared.

When Hise returned with the treaty, Polk tabled it, left the presidency, and died. His successor, Zachary Taylor, sent another envoy to Nicaragua, Ephraim George Squier, whose main qualifi-

---

[10] Bemis, *Diplomatic History*, p. 247.

cation for the job was that as the author of *The Moundbuilders of the Mississippi Valley*, the outstanding work of its kind, he had an interest in Central American archeology. He was also a Whig, but a Whig expansionist. As a person, Squier was exceedingly interesting. The foremost American archeologist of his time, he used his diplomatic missions to Central and South America to do research on a series of books about those regions which are still classics. Almost forgotten, however, is his important *The Serpent Symbol and the Worship of the Reciprocal Principles of Nature in America*, which clearly anticipated the work of Carl Jung if not Sigmund Freud.

Squier was a globe-trotter and friend of John Lloyd Stephens, another American diplomat who once bought the Mayan city of Copan for fifty dollars; of Brantz Mayer, consul to Mexico and recorder of its history; of John Russell Bartlett, the United States Mexican Boundary Commissioner; and of Edgar Allan Poe. Later in his career Squier married the notorious Mrs. Frank Leslie, publisher of the celebrated magazine *Frank Leslie's Illustrated Weekly*. He went out in a blaze of glory when, after a riotous night in a New Orleans brothel, carefully prearranged by his spouse, who had fallen in love with Joaquin Miller, "the Poet of the Sierras," he was hailed into court and "convicted" of adultery.[11] Divorced, disenfranchised, penniless, with no more exotic places to visit, Squier went instead to an asylum and uneventfully died. Such was the man that "Old Rough and Ready" sent to Central America to confront the British.

In Central America, Squier engaged in a strange diplomatic duel with his British counterpart, Frederick Chatfield. On September 28, 1849, Squier signed a treaty with Honduras that gave the United States Tigre Island, key to the Pacific outlet of any Nicaraguan canal route. Chatfield, a wily strategist, retaliated by signing a treaty with Costa Rica—ever to be a thorn in the side of Nicaragua. The Briton also seized Tigre Island. Squier then negotiated a treaty which granted the United States the right to build a canal and transit line across Nicaragua. Meanwhile the British government disavowed Chatfield's invasion of Tigre Island and hauled down its flag.

---

[11]Madeleine B. Stern, *Purple Passage: the Life of Mrs. Frank Leslie* (Norman, Okla.: University of Oklahoma Press, 1953), pp. 63–64.

All this time, the Whig President Taylor and his successor kept on the table a mounting stack of Central American treaties, while Secretary of State, John M. Clayton, in an unfortunate candid moment divulged his conviction that Monroe's Doctrine was not gospel. Britain was therefore anxious to negotiate a Central American treaty with him in particular, and sent Sir Henry Bulwer armed with full negotiating powers, across the Atlantic by fast packet. With the Monroe Doctrine not being invoked, nothing stood in the way of an amicable agreement between the two great powers. On April 19, 1850, they concluded the Clayton-Bulwer Treaty—a diplomatic defeat for the United States, and a stunning British victory.

The Clayton-Bulwer Treaty superseded the Hise, Squier, and Bidlack treaties. It declared that "neither government would ever obtain or maintain for itself any exclusive control over any ship canal through any part of Central America; nor fortify the same in the vicinity thereof nor colonize or assume any dominion over Central America." Neither country would make use of any existing alliance or treaty with the Central American countries to fortify or hold any advantage of the right of isthmian commerce or navigation over any other. Since the United States by this time held transit treaties with New Grenada, Nicaragua, Honduras, Mexico, and the friendship of Guatemala, while Britain held only the Mosquito Coast and a treaty with Costa Rica, the adage "hands across the sea" seemed less than a fair exchange. Particularly did it seem so when the diplomats quietly turned the Monroe Doctrine face down and agreed that Britain could keep Belize, the Bay Islands, and its protectorate over the poor Indians of the Mosquito Coast. The Mosquito Coast, especially, proved to be a trouble spot and in 1854, because of the belligerence of the "Mosquitoans" to transit passengers and shippers, Captain Hollins of the United States Sloop *Cyane* was obliged to level Greytown to the ground. In the long run, however, the spirit of the Clayton-Bulwer Treaty was highly important. The two great maritime nations had formally established the principle that the main arteries of world commerce should be open to ships of all nations, and adopting this principle of neutrality had avoided still another bloody showdown on one of the world's frontiers. The same principle was later applied to Suez, though it has since been abandoned.

III

The Clayton-Bulwer Treaty, however, was merely the beginning of skirmish and competition in Central America. In the decade of the fifties all diplomatic relations and niceties were severely tested. While the struggle over the Mosquito Coast was proceeding, American entrepreneurs began to venture into all parts of Central America, from southern Mexico to Atrato below Panama. Among the first of these ventures was that of the Panama Railway Company chartered by New York State at a capitalization of $1 million. Along with this, and in association with it, William K. Aspinwall organized the Pacific Mail Steamship Company and obtained a federal contract for transporting mail, troops, and other government baggage to California by way of the Isthmus of Panama. Taking advantage of the treaty with New Grenada, the company employed Captain George W. Hughes of the Corps of Topographical Engineers to run a survey for the railroad across Panama. Then, in 1850, it established headquarters in Panama and began construction of the road. The railroad builders experienced many difficulties with swampy jungle terrain; two contracting firms defaulted. Imported laborers from Europe and the Far East died by the thousands from yellow fever, but by 1855 Aspinwall's company had established ports on either end of the line, with railroad repair depots and with steamers plying the lakes, and it had completed the required 43 miles of track across the Isthmus. In the five years between December, 1854, and December, 1859, Robert Russel has pointed out, the company carried 196,000 passengers, $300 million worth of bullion, and 100,000 bags of mail.[12] By 1860, because of the failure of all the other Isthmian enterprises, the Panama Railroad Company and the associated Aspinwall and Vanderbilt steamship lines held a monopoly over all Central American traffic.

If the Panama Railroad Company was the very model of a successful, although difficult enterprise, the trans-Isthmian efforts in Nicaragua proved to be the opposite. Because British bankers, out of nationalistic motives, refused to subscribe funds for the construction of a joint British-American Nicaraguan Canal, Amer-

---

[12]Robert Russel, *Communication With the Pacific Coast as an Issue in American Politics, 1783–1864* (Cedar Rapids, Iowa: The Torch Press, 1948), p. 61.

ican entrepreneurs were forced to resort to other expedients. As early as 1850 Commodore Vanderbilt sent steamships to San Juan (renamed Greytown) to establish first rights to the proposed canal. Failing to get the required funds in England, however, he sent his agent Joseph L. White to Nicaragua to negotiate a separate agreement that would allow Vanderbilt's firm, the Accessory Transit Company, to begin transportation of passengers across Nicaragua independently of the construction of the canal. In 1851 he secured such an agreement from one of two governments claiming legitimate rule over Nicaragua.

By the end of 1851 Vanderbilt had his line in operation. Two small steamboats plied the river above Greytown. Two other vessels were put into operation on Lake Nicaragua, and a macadamized road was built between the lake and the Pacific over which passenger coaches were pulled through jungle and mountain valleys. At either end of the line he had ocean vessels to take passengers to California or points east. Generally it was an efficient, although complicated, operation that depended upon the good will of a stable government in Nicaragua. Such a resolute government did not exist, and Vanderbilt's enterprise was built at great risk, particularly given the impending competition from Aspinwall in Panama, and British attempts to obstruct his efforts at the port of entry, Greytown. It was these efforts, disavowed by the home government, that called forth the drastic action of Captain Hollins and the *Cyane* in 1854.

The outstanding aspect of Nicaragua was its instability. In addition to the British intrusion on the Mosquito Coast, two major factions were vying for control of the government, the Liberals and the Legitimists. It was a situation ripe for adventurers, and they did not fail to appear. In 1854, Thomas L. Kinney, a Texan entrepreneur, and former owner of the steamboat *Yellowstone*, which contributed so much to Sam Houston's victory at San Jacinto, showed up on the Mosquito Coast. He had formed "the Central American Agricultural and Mining Association" a thinly veiled front for a freebooter's attempt at control of strife-ridden Nicaragua. His partners were highly placed individuals in the United States government, though Secretary of State William L. Marcy, an honest man, served notice on Kinney that no attempts at filibustering would be countenanced. Kinney, however, proved to be the most timid of adventurers. When in June of 1855 William Walker appeared in Nicaragua with his band of fifty veteran ruffians and served notice that if he found Kinney in the territory he would hang him, Kinney immediately gave up his grand plan and returned to the safer confines of Texas.

The most colorful if not disgraceful period of Nicaraguan history began with the arrival of Walker. A slight man, five feet five inches tall, with light yellow hair, white eyebrows, and cold grey eyes set in a freckled, mummified face, Walker's appearance hardly betrayed the reckless and deadly individual that he was. An educated man with an M.D. from the University of Pennsylvania and several years of study in Paris, plus years of reading law in New Orleans, Walker succumbed all too readily to the romantic spirit of the times. He had drifted to San Francisco in the Gold Rush, and then suddenly in 1853 he led an ill-fated filibustering expedition into Sonora, which very nearly wrecked the delicate negotiations in progress that culminated in the Gadsden Purchase.

Somehow Walker survived his Sonoran debacle. When in June, 1855, he and his fifty "immortals" landed at Realjo on the Pacific Coast of Nicaragua, they were welcomed by representatives of the Liberal faction, enlisted in the "army of liberation," and began the strenuous campaign for Nicaragua. Although it caused concern, there was little that Britain or the United States could do, at the time, to stop Walker, since he was invited into the country by the Liberal faction. Walker professed to be much impressed by Nicaragua, "for which," as he put it, "nature has done much and man little." He determined to work hard for both the cause of liberation and for an empire. Almost immediately he and his men overwhelmed the Legitimist stronghold of Rivas in a bloody frontal assault. From that point on there ensued a series of attacks, counterattacks, and fierce battles, all of which Walker and his men miraculously won. Particularly noteworthy was the battle of Virgin Bay of September 3, 1845, in which he annihilated a force of 600 drunken Legitimist soldiers who made a surprise attack on his army. His master stroke, however, was the capture, while its defenders were marching on Rivas, of Granada, the Legitimist capital. Capturing Granada, he became master of Nicaragua by virtue of the fact that he held all of the families of the Legitimists as hostages.

After Granada, Walker began receiving direct aid from Vanderbilt's steamship company whose vessels carried reinforcements and supplies to his army—making his military position impregnable. The Legitimists surrendered, and a puppet government was formed with Patricio Rivas, actually a former Legitimist, as figurehead. Walker, as commander of the army, held the real power in time-honored Latin fashion. The Rivas government was recognized by the American Minister Wheeler, although Marcy immediately disavowed his action. Back in the United States public opinion supported Walker, who was regarded by many as a kind of Sam Houston come to rescue the Isthmus from the British for the forces of republican democracy. Actually he was a dictator, and as soon as he could he sent Rivas packing out of the country.

As dictator Walker proved to be a poor political strategist. Heady with his newly acquired power, he sought recognition for his government, while at the same time he menaced and outraged virtually every nation and interest he came in touch with. His first and gravest mistake was to abrogate the transit contract with Vanderbilt and confiscate his ships for the Nicaraguan government. This antagonized Vanderbilt tremendously. It also made it nearly impossible for Walker to get any further reinforcements and supplies for his army. Then, seeking aid from his friends in the South at the suggestion of Pierre Soulé, he introduced slavery into Nicaragua. This forever destroyed his republican and democratic pose. From that time on, every hand was against him, and with his slowly weakening army he fought repeated battles against an international brigade composed of "volunteers" from all Central American nations, particularly Costa Rica and Guatemala. The Central American international brigade was largely supplied with arms from Britain and was commanded by "advisors" from the British regular army. To Britain Walker represented a grave threat to any plan for economic exploitation of Central America, and that country cynically aided Costa Rica in its attempts to gain control of the canal route.[13]

---

[13] Albert Z. Carr, *The World and William Walker* (New York, Evanston, and London: Harper and Row, 1963), pp. 214–218.

The end of November, 1857, found Walker besieged in his capital, Granada, by an overwhelming allied army. Defeat was inevitable, and the "grey eyed man of destiny" ordered the total destruction of the city and prepared to fight a last-ditch battle before leaving the country. The battle for Granada lasted nearly three weeks, but Walker's army was destroyed along with the city. As Walker and the remnants of his force sailed on the steamer *Virgen* from the ruined city, his lieutenant, General Henningson, just before boarding the ship, thrust a lance into the ground. A note was written on a piece of rawhide attached to the lance, which said defiantly, *Aqui fué Granada*—"Here was Granada."[14] The destruction of the city symbolized the havoc he had wreaked on Nicaragua. And although he tried twice more, Walker could never return to the country he had once commanded. Ultimately he was captured in a futile attempt to "liberate" Honduras, and his captor, Salmon, a British naval officer, in violation of the terms of surrender, turned Walker over to the Honduran authorities who had him shot and mutilated on September 12, 1860.[15] The Walker episode represented the extreme of reckless, romantic American expansionism. It also suggested, however, that (similar to the struggle over California and Texas) the conflict between Walker and the Central American factions was not the most important one. Behind the opposition to Walker lay the desire of the American capitalist, Vanderbilt, to gain a monopoly of isthmian transit routes. And beyond this lay the determination of Great Britain to contain American economic and political expansion in Central America by any means. The fate of the Central American countries themselves was incidental.

In the end Buchanan, anxious to placate the British with a civil war impending, disavowed Walker and allowed Nicaragua to become a virtual British protectorate. Although he was a scoundrel and the bête noire of American capitalists and English imperialists, William Walker, the Central American filibuster, was a representative international figure of his time—the romantic age of Clive and Napoleon and Chinese Gordon. Perhaps the magazine, *Harper's*, put it best: "Had William Walker been an Englishman or a Frenchman, he would never have become a 'filibuster,' but

[14] Wallace, *Destiny and Glory*, p. 229.
[15] Carr, *The World and William Walker*, pp. 270–272.

would have found ample scope for his extraordinary talents in the legitimate service of his country."[16]

IV

After the downfall of Walker, however, a new diplomatic order was restored in Central America, although not without a struggle. A French adventurer persuaded Costa Rica to claim the Nicaraguan canal route, and this affair was only smoothed over by the Cass-Yrisarri Treaty of 1858. This in turn called forth the Ouseley Mission by the British to Central America, and Ouseley, backed by a British offer to abrogate the Clayton-Bulwer Treaty entirely, openly threatened war for the control of the Isthmus. Finally, however, in a series of treaties signed by Britain, France, and the United States with the various Central American countries, most of the differences were settled, and all parties were insured territorial integrity and free rights of transit across the Isthmus. Just as the Civil War loomed on the horizon, the Central American question was resolved. Private adventurism was virtually over. The Panama Railroad Company, Aspinwall, and Vanderbilt had their monopoly, and Britain, France, and the United States had each contained one another's expansion. The classic situation of balance of power had been achieved.

V

The other diplomatic events of the period, those relating to Mexico, seem almost anticlimactic, but they have a certain importance. Starting in 1844, Mexico granted a series of rights to cross the Tehuantepec Isthmus, first to one of its own citizens, Jose de Garay, then to Peter A. Hargous, who represented a New York banking firm, and ultimately to a New Orleans combine headed by A. G. Sloo. Throughout the fifties, the Sloo and Hargous claimants contested with each other and Mexico resisted the attempts by the American government to secure guarantees for either of the claimants, especially if the guarantee involved the right to protect any proposed canal or railway by American armed force.

The United States began, in 1850, to concentrate on possible

---

[16]Quoted in *Ibid.*, p. 274. See also p. 272 for a comparison of Walker with Clive and Napoleon.

transcontinental railroad routes within its own boundaries. Senator Benton, the exponent of a central United States railroad to the Pacific, stated that he wished no arrangements "which are to keep me out of my own country one moment beyond the time we are able to finish our road."[17] Laying a railroad across the United States, however, proved more difficult than at first imagined. The members of the United States Boundary Commission discovered that because of the use of Disturnell's erroneous map and Trist's ambiguous wording of the Treaty of Guadalupe Hidalgo, the southern border of the United States ran just north of the only passes through the southern Rockies suitable for a railroad. And since it was thought at the time that any practicable transcontinental railroad would have to run across Texas and through the Southwest, a Congressional clamor arose, headed by Texans and Southwesterners. They claimed that the Whig Boundary Commissioner, John R. Bartlett, had made an error in interpreting

[17]Quoted in Russel, *Communication*, p. 58.

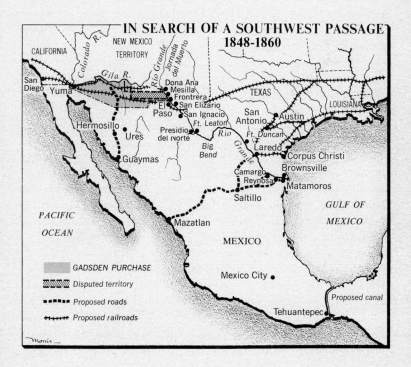

Trist's treaty with regard to the southern boundary of New Mexico; but in fact, according to Trist's own interpretation, obscured by the clamor, Bartlett had not. Out of the Democratic furor in Congress, however, and New Mexican Governor William C. Lane's aggressive action in occupying the Mesilla Valley and other disputed territory, grew the sentiment for an additional purchase of land in the Southwest. James Gadsden of South Carolina was sent to Mexico on July 15, 1853, to purchase one last slice of Mexican territory—as much of a slice as he could get, even Lower California if possible.

Gadsden had to deal with a man hard pressed for cash, as usual —General Santa Anna. But even so, Santa Anna refused to sell more territory than was needed for the road. Finally, on December 30, 1853, Gadsden made the purchase that rounded out the present southern boundary of the United States. The price was $15 million (later reduced to $10 million) and an additional $5 million in liabilities to the Garay claimants. After a secret debate in the Senate and an open, acrimonious debate over the appropriation in the House in April and May led by northern opponents of a southern transcontinental railroad, the treaty was finally ratified on June 29, 1854.

As it turned out, where the railroad was concerned, the purchase was useless. Returning to the United States from his Mexican negotiations, General Gadsden was stopped by an inept customs official who demanded to search his baggage. Indignantly, Gadsden replied, "I, sir, am General Gadsden, and there is nothing in my trunk but my treaty."[18] Indeed. The Pacific Railroad Surveys of 1853, authorized by Secretary of War Jefferson Davis, officially proclaimed the 32nd parallel or extreme southwestern line the most superior transcontinental railroad route. But a close inspection of the reports indicated that at least two routes, one along the 35th and another along the 41st parallel (near the actual Union Pacific-Central Pacific routes) were superior to that of the 32nd parallel. This was particularly true for two reasons: (1) San Francisco, now the burgeoning port that everyone predicted, had come to be the western focal point of any transcontinental line, and (2) General Gadsden had stopped just short in

---

[18]Quoted in Paul Neff Garber, *The Gadsden Treaty* (Philadelphia: University of Pennsylvania Press, 1923), p. 107.

his geographic surgery at the western end of the line and failed to purchase the site of the crucial pass into San Diego. Even today the Southern Pacific is forced to dip briefly into Mexico on its line into the California port. The land acquired in Gadsden's purchase has become valuable and important for other reasons today, but as far as the railroad was concerned he, indeed, "had nothing in his trunk but his treaty."

With Gadsden's Purchase, however, and with the series of adventures in the Caribbean culminating in the agreements of 1859, American expansion in the western hemisphere came to a close for a time. The expansionist urge had not entirely ended, however. During the Civil War the French, confirming long-held American fears, seized the opportunity to occupy Mexico, while William Seward and American expansionists looked longingly toward Canada and Alaska.

There remains one final chapter in the diplomacy of the Manifest Destiny period, but it is an important one in the light of the mid-twentieth century. This is the story of the American advance across the Pacific into the Far East and to the South Seas. With that adventure, American aspirations, conceived on a Humboldtean scale, indeed came full circle around the globe.

CHAPTER VI

Looking Westward 'Crost the Sea

ONE OF THE MAGNETS that drew Americans across the continent to the Pacific shores was the myth that the riches of the world were lying dormant in China—that remote empire revealed to the West by Marco Polo—and in the exotic templed countries of the Far East from the Indian subcontinent to the Spice Islands of Java and Sumatra. This image of remote and fabled riches, so dear to the American romantic imagination, rested once again, like the whole concept of empire, on European history and tradition. It conjured up visions of De Gama, Magellan, Marco Polo, Mendez Pinto the Portuguese, the bejeweled Sultans of Sulu, Malay Pirates, and the rich trade routes to the Spice Islands and India that Columbus had set out to find. These routes, which passed through the Indian Ocean and the Red Sea, had lasted for a thousand years and had contributed mightily to the rise of Moslem and European civilization.

The American image of the East rested, in short, upon the revelations of the great Age of Discovery, but it was compounded also of myths and some additional facts. The irresistible Western drive to the Far East became part of the whole romantic urge to reach out to the remote and marvelous corners of the globe, the belief that somewhere, over the horizon, beyond the ken of ordinary rational man, lay some sublime truth, and the possible meaning of human existence. In the early nineteenth century philosophies of the mystic East became the vogue among romantics both in Europe and in America. Even a casual perusal of the works of Emerson and Thoreau attests to this. Equally important, the mysterious East had Biblical and Christian meaning that attached itself to the imaginations of men. It was the ancestral home of man as God had put him on the earth, and somehow the point of origin demanded a return—an Aristotelian completeness, a fulfillment of prophecy, or in modern parlance a "return to the womb" of mankind.

In addition an important contributing factor to renewed American and European interest in the Far East was the work of seaborne global explorers in the late eighteenth century, exemplified by Captain Cook, whose patient collection of facts and exotic specimens from the remote regions of the South Seas and the Far East suddenly expanded the tightly structured and rational Western mind to the unlimited horizon of romanticism. Thus when Western men looked to the East, their exotic impressions were reinforced by scientific authority. After Cook the best of these authorities at the beginning of the nineteenth century, indeed the giant of the age, Alexander von Humboldt, envisioned the inevitable progress of Europe and America westward to the Far East along an isothermal or climatic belt that ran around the globe through the temperate zone. His scientific works, written in a highly romantic vein, provided inspiration for countless effusions of rhetoric by American expansionists. William Gilpin the visionary first governor of Colorado advocated a global railroad heading west across the Continent to Siberia, China, and India. William Seward, a normally cautious Whig politician became the leading American expansionist of the mid-nineteenth century. His interests, too, were centered in the Far East and northward to Alaska.

Tradition, history, fable, philosophy, Christianity, mystery, and science all contributed to the magnetism of the East in the mid-nineteenth century. But there was one thing more—the economic motive. New England sea traders headed south around the Horn and the Cape of Good Hope bound for the East. They searched for spices and silks and sandalwood, and later they hunted whales, charting their courses around the world. In short, they risked much—loneliness, discomfort, and death—for the profit that made Salem and Boston and Nantucket for a time civilized crossroads of the world. Thus the attraction of the East was both rational and irrational, and it came to be laced with some of the same insecurities and fears of foreign competition that spurred American continental and Caribbean expansion. Taken together, all of these complex motives made it inevitable that at the high tide of Manifest Destiny, as an expression of their culture, Americans would look "Westward 'crost the sea."

I

By the second half of the eighteenth century, ships from the American colonies had already penetrated the mysterious East, and shortly after the securing of independence, consuls authorized by the Articles of Confederation government were sent out to posts in Calcutta and Canton. In 1785 the first large American cargo ship to journey to East Asia, *The Empress of China*, arrived in Canton and trade with the Celestial Empire began in earnest. On the other side of the world, far from Eastern Seaboard America, the earliest American traders were at a distinct disadvantage. Moreover, the hostile and exclusive policy of China limited penetration from the outside world to the port of Canton. Nevertheless, assisted by their British and French counterparts, the Yankee traders rapidly widened their base of trade in the Orient.

The earliest profitable trade was developed by the sea otter traders of Bryant, Sturgis & Company of Boston. These traders sent their vessels to the Northwest coast of America, secured furs from the Indians, and carried them across the Pacific to China. Often they stopped at Hawaii to repair their ships and take on a load of valuable sandalwood. In China they traded furs and sandalwood for silks, nankeens, procelains, and other desirable goods; then they headed back around the Cape of Good Hope to New England. By the time he became head of his company, William Sturgis had made five such voyages around the world. Soon, speculators from New York such as John Jacob Astor entered the trade and, like the British and the New Englanders, these speculators began to engage in the profitable sideline of opium trading with India and China.

Bold sea ventures to the Orient were not without risk, however. In 1802 the entire crew, save two, of the brig *Boston* was massacred by Indians on the Northwest Coast and their heads displayed in grisly triumph on the quarterdeck. One of Astor's ships in 1811 was likewise overwhelmed by coastal savages, and its last survivor set a match to the powder magazine and blew the whole ship to kingdom come—with two-hundred Indian conquerors aboard. Other mariners were attacked by pirates off Java or shipwrecked in the cold northern seas off Japan. But still they came on in ever greater numbers until the Embargo and the War of 1812 curtailed their activities.

During the War of 1812 Captain David Porter, cruising the Pacific aboard the United States frigate *Essex*, conducted highly successful raids on British shipping. But also during his cruise, he paused, in 1813, to claim the island of Nukahiva in the South Pacific for the United States. This island had been discovered by the American Captain Joseph Ingraham in 1791, and when Porter pulled in for repairs at the island (later to be made famous by Melville's *Typee*) he erected a fort named after President Madison, rechristened the harbor Massachusetts Bay, concluded a treaty of annexation, and then sailed away never to return. His action was later disavowed by the United States government, and after years of neglect, the island was officially annexed by France in 1833.

By 1820 the United States had established consuls at Ile de France in French Mauritius, Batavia in Java, Manila in the Philippines, and Honolulu in the Sandwich Islands (now the Hawaiian Islands). In 1826 Captain Thomas Ap Catesby Jones, who was to make such a serious blunder at Monterey, California in 1842, cruised the Pacific and concluded provisional treaties with the chiefs of Tahiti, the Society Islands, and Hawaii. These treaties related to the rights of stranded American sailors and deserters or mutineers.

The first official American diplomat to go to the Far East was Edmund Roberts, who was sent by President Andrew Jackson in 1831 to accompany Captain Edmund Fanning's cruise around the world at the head of a small squadron of three ships led by the U. S. frigate *Potomac*. Also on board was Jeremiah N. Reynolds, author of the whaling story "Mocha Dick," the prototype for Melville's whaling epic, *Moby Dick*. As a result of his voyage on the *Potomac*, Reynolds became the chief promoter of an official United States exploring expedition to the South Seas. As the diplomatic representative, Roberts' mission was to negotiate treaties with Siam, Cochin China, Muscat, and Japan. He failed to get his treaty with Cochin China, but he signed agreements with Siam and the Sultan of Muscat and Zanzibar. Before he could get to Japan, however, Roberts died in Macao in 1836.

After he had returned from his round-the-world voyage, Reynolds addressed Congress in a speech that lasted three hours and was one-hundred pages long, urging an official United States Government expedition to the Pacific similar to those conducted by the British. His argument was bolstered by the fact that, since 1819, when young Nathaniel Palmer, a sea otter hunter from Stonington, Connecticut, discovered Antarctica, there had been unusual curiosity in New England about the existence of land in far southern latitudes. Reynolds was further backed by all the whalers and traders who had plied the Pacific for years, and by ex-President John Quincy Adams. As a result of Reynolds' efforts Captain Charles Wilkes left Norfolk, Virginia, in 1838 with six ships of the United States Exploring Expedition. His voyage, one of the two most important in the early nineteenth century, resulted in the discovery of the Antarctic from which the present American claim derives. Wilkes also cruised the South Seas, landing at Pago Pago in Samoa and concluded a treaty with its native chief which later was the foundation for an American claim to that island. During his voyage Wilkes mapped and visited most of the major South Pacific island groups—the Marquesas, Fiji, the Gilberts, the Marshalls, Midway, and Hawaii. The importance of his voyage to Puget Sound and the Northwest coast of America has been related earlier. On his return to America, Wilkes stopped at Canton and all of the other major outposts in the Far East. Unfortunately, when he returned in 1841, the magnificent results of his voyage were obscured by petty bickering and the studied ignorance of President Tyler who personally disliked him.

The Anglo-Chinese, or Opium War of 1839-42, was the direct cause of the first American treaty with China. This conflict arose because the Chinese Emperor attempted to prevent the importation of British Indian opium into China by means of the Canton trading establishments. British warships blockaded China, and American interests were severely threatened, particularly after the British had forced the Emperor to sign the Treaty of Nanking granting them unrestricted trading rights in five south China ports and the outright cession of Hong Kong. President Tyler, as quickly as he could, sent Caleb Cushing as minister plenipotentiary to China, and Cushing in 1844 succeeded in getting the Treaty of Wanghia, which opened the ports of Canton, Amoy, Ningpo,

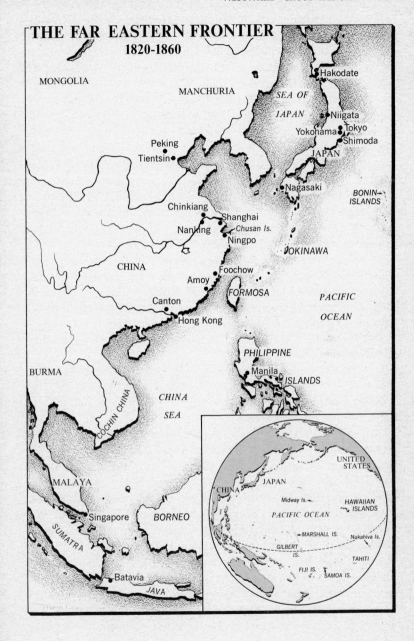

THE FAR EASTERN FRONTIER
1820-1860

Foochow, and Shanghai to American merchants on terms as favorable as those granted to the British. The Americans, however, neither demanded nor received any Chinese territory.

The basis for Cushing's treaty was the Treaty of Nanking, between China and Britain which contained the provision, inserted by the Chinese, that equal trading rights would be granted to all nations if they desired them. This, of course, forms the basis for the later so-called Open Door Policy which later became American dogma. The significance of the Wanghia Treaty is that, with the exception of Hong Kong, the United States, unlike England, desired no Chinese territory. That is, the American government desired trading rights but no political responsibility in China. In later years Britain continually departed from this policy, acquiring Singapore, Burma, and Malaya, which in turn, as world affairs developed and Anglo-American alliances were cemented, committed the United States to a political intervention in the Far East even if the Philippines had never been acquired. Also significant is the fact that the Open Door Policy was essentially a Chinese strategem to protect itself by increasing the number of competing traders, hence creating factions, which, in a spirit reminiscent of Madison's Tenth Federalist Paper, might be expected to cancel each other out.

II

After 1850, because of the settlement of California and the acquisition of Isthmian routes, American interest in the Far East and the Pacific reached a peak. In addition, the invention of ocean-going steamships changed the focus of diplomatic objectives. Before the age of steam, trading posts, or outfitting posts, were sufficient, but with the new technology the need for coaling stations in the form of secure island possessions became apparent. The acquisition of such stations would bring with it increased diplomatic competition, and a heretofore unneeded political and military commitment to the remote regions of the Far East.

Commodore Matthew C. Perry was the greatest exponent of permanent American commitment to the Far East. He sailed for Japan in 1852, after having made a careful study of the requirements of steamship navigation in the Pacific. In sailing, he had as his objective to secure proper coaling stations as stepping stones across the Pacific. World competition with England demanded them. Perry wrote in a dispatch from Madeira:

When we look at the possessions in the east of our great maritime rival England and of the constant and rapid increase of their fortified ports, we should be admonished of the necessity of prompt measures on our part. . . . Fortunately the Japanese and many other islands in the Pacific are still left untouched by this unconscionable government; and as some of them lay in a route of commerce which is destined to become of great importance to the United States, no time should be lost in adopting active measures to secure a sufficient number of ports of refuge.[1]

Perry's specific plan was to open feudal Japan to American commerce and to secure control over bases on the Bonin Islands, Okinawa, and Formosa. When he arrived off Tokyo Bay on July 8, 1853, with his flotilla of warships, Perry left a letter from President Fillmore to be delivered to the Japanese emperor calling for a peace treaty, and then sailed away to seize, as he had planned, the Bonin Islands and a coaling station on Okinawa. In the latter operation he signed a treaty with the local authorities for trading, coaling, and seamen's rights that was ratified by the United States Senate in 1854. However, most of his proposals for territorial aggrandizement in the Far East were rejected by the American government.

In the spring Perry returned to Japan and, through firm but skillful diplomacy, secured a treaty of friendship on March 31, 1854, which opened the ports of Hakodota and Shimoda to Americans. While it was not quite the grand conquest of Asia and the Pacific that he had hoped for, it was the beginning of Japan's remarkable emergence from the dark ages of feudalism and therefore one of the most important, although ambiguous, events in world history.

Perry's opening of Japan was followed by a further series of treaties, similar to those with China, which Japan granted to Britain, Holland, and Russia as the Japanese made full commitment to the outside world. The opening of Japan was also followed by the establishment of an American consul, Townsend Harris, in Japan in 1856. This individual, surely one of the greatest of Ameri-

---

[1] Quoted in Foster Rhea Dulles, *America in the Pacific* (Boston and New York: Houghton Mifflin Co., 1938), p. 67.

can diplomats, by means of forthrightness and the skillful use of the Russian menace, painted as the colossus of the north, convinced the Japanese that a full alliance and exchange of ministers with the United States would protect them from falling into the same situation as China. It would give them knowledge of new technology so as to enable them to take their place as one of the powers of the modern world. He made clear, however, that the United States would put no pressure on Japan to achieve these goals. It would have to be a free decision, but if she chose to accept an American alliance, Harris predicted, "Japan will become the England of the Orient."[2] In 1858 he secured his treaty, with full consular and ministerial exchanges. And in 1860 the first Japanese ambassador arrived in Washington. Politically, culturally, (even strategically), this event far overshadowed the later American decision to acquire the Philippines. Long before that insular possession became a hostage to Japan, Townsend Harris had put feudal Japan on the road to its own "manifest destiny," whereby it would be in a position to hold the Philippines as hostage and along with it much of Asia. The American treaty with Japan began a chain reaction that committed the United States, in an irrevocable way, to the destiny of Asia.

While Townsend Harris was working in Japan, Dr. Peter Parker, the American commissioner in China, was attempting to complete the annexation of Formosa. He was spurred on to this activity by the attempts of Britain and France to widen their trading wedges in China. His plan was to cooperate with the British and the French in seizing Chinese territory as a means of forcing China into treaty revision. Britain was to have Chusan, France, Korea; and the United States, Formosa. These territories would be held until the emperor made "proper" agreements with the European nations. Parker naively wrote home that he hoped "the Government of the United States may not *shrink* from the *action* which the interests of humanity, civilization, navigation, and commerce impose upon it."[3]

Parker urged annexation while working in collusion with two American traders, W. M. Robinet and Gideon Nye, Jr., who had constructed a port on Formosa, raised an American flag over the

[2] Bemis, *Diplomatic History*, p. 360.
[3] Dulles, *America in the Pacific*, p. 76.

port, and by 1856 had loaded about 78 vessels with cargoes at an estimated value of $50 thousand. He also enlisted the aid of Commodore James Armstrong, commander of the United States Pacific Squadron. In a final dispatch to Washington he pleaded:

Great Britain has her St. Helena in the Atlantic, her Gibralter and Malta in the Mediterranean, her Aden in the Red Sea, Mauritius, Ceylon, Penang and Singapore in the Indian Ocean, and Hongkong in the China seas. If the United States is so disposed, and can *arrange* for the cession of Formosa, England certainly cannot object.[4]

(One wonders, however, about the Formosans, but perhaps not for long.)

The ultimate result of Parker's adventure was his recall and his replacement by William Reed, who went out to the East with explicit instructions not to work for the annexation of any territory. In similar fashion Commodore Rodgers, who had succeeded Cadwallader Ringgold as commander of the North Pacific Exploring Expedition, was rebuffed when he sought to "explore" the islands off northern Japan for possible American outposts. He was advised that funds were exhausted and commanded to return home.

Joint British and French belligerency was the final event that was significant to America with respect to China and resulted in the new Treaty of Tientsin secured in 1858. This treaty broadened the number of trading ports to eleven, granted religious toleration, and allowed the Europeans to send missions to Peking. It completed the capitulation of Imperial China, opening the way for a horde of missionaries and civilizers. The United States became a full participant in this treaty and hence before 1860 bore responsibilities of some consequence in China which, in turn, created a tradition that perforce elicited the later misplaced sympathies of John Hay.

In the Far East the United States pursued a curious love-hate relationship with its maritime rivals Britain and France. Because of pressure from the American trading interests, the United States government was forced to do what it could to make the American traders competitive with their rivals. In so doing, except in the matter of the opium trade, and Townsend Harris's forthright dealings with Japan, the United States largely followed

---

[4] *Ibid.*, p. 77.

the British and French example. In a mad scramble for wealth, although not for territory, the United States became a ruthless economic imperialist in the fashion of Britain and France. Had it not been intimidated by the greater experience of these nations and by their example, had the desire for maritime wealth been controlled with the same vigor as the desire for territorial aggrandizement, the United States in later years might have escaped being "tarred with the same brush" of imperialism that has blackened with guilt its far more active and successful European rivals. In this case the American tendency always to adopt European ways was most unfortunate.

III

On the American road across the Pacific rested the Hawaiian Islands, and across that strategic kingdom ran another of those world frontiers of commercial and diplomatic rivalry. Discovered by Captain Cook in 1778, the islands had been strangely overlooked by the Spanish Manila galleons of the sixteenth century. From the time of their discovery by Cook, the Hawaiian Islands became a favored stopping place of seafarers from all nations—a place of orgy and delight as well as a source of fruitful commerce in sandalwood. Then in 1820 American missionaries arrived in Honolulu and a period of strife descended upon the island. Gradually the missionaries became landowners and advisors to the native king. By 1849 the Reverend Richard Armstrong, having largely abandoned his missionary duties, was being pensioned by the King of Hawaii, and had acquired some 600 acres of choice land. In 1850 he held 1800 acres. Two years later, ten of his fellow clergymen had secured an average of 400 acres apiece. These men gradually rose in power and importance, but their desire, unlike that of the Texans, was not to annex themselves to the United States. In control of the central government, and hence the economic opportunity, they preferred independence until such time as they were threatened by a greater power. Then, of course, they would capitulate; they, indeed, would "come to the bower."

First the British, in 1836, then in 1839 the French, signed treaties guaranteeing the integrity of Hawaii. The United States showed little official interest as late as 1842 when further treaties were negotiated with the twin maritime powers. But in 1843, jealous over American economic success in the Islands, the British consul, a naval commander, Captain George Paulet, took over the kingdom for five months until his action was disavowed by Britain. In 1849 the French ostensibly took umbrage at the exclusion of Catholic missionaries from the Islands and with a flotilla of warships took virtual control of Hawaii for two years, or until the home government also disavowed them.

Subsequently, in 1854, fearing the consequences of a continued rivalry to their investment, threatened by a possible insurrection, and alarmed by rumors of a proposed filibustering expedition to be led by William Walker from San Francisco, the missionary party finally proposed annexation to the United States. They proposed, however, immediate statehood as the price of annexation, and the Pierce administration was not willing to grant this. Secretary of State Marcy therefore rejected the treaty proposal. Prince Alexander succeeded King Kamehameha III as ruler of Hawaii and, being strongly in favor of independence, stopped all negotiations with the United States and relied upon the "territorial integrity" agreements of 1842. Thus the United States voluntarily checked its drive to the west (with the exception of Alaska) until the end of the nineteenth century, content to rest with a stalemate across the mid-Pacific frontier. America had emerged as an important world power in the decades of Manifest Destiny, but during the 1850's it reached the limits of its "destiny." Balance of power in North America was destroyed; containment pushed far out to sea. At last, on the eve of the Civil War, a kind of equilibrium and some fleeting sense of security appeared to have been achieved.

Epilogue

T HE ROAR OF the batteries in Charleston harbor on April 12, 1861, proved conclusively that security was only an illusion, at best achieved temporarily and then at the price of courage and struggle. For the next four years the United States was to be engaged in preserving the continental union that had grown out of sixty years of unrelenting conflict and crisis dating back to the birth of the Republic and the first dreams of empire. While internal strife preoccupied Americans, France moved into Mexico, and Britain waited, uncertain until 1863 as to which side, North or South, was to be victorious and hence deserving of its support. Once, in a terrible blunder, Captain Charles Wilkes with his capture of the *Trent*, nearly drove Britain into the arms of the South; but she waited. Despite all the prewar protestations against slavery, despite the fact that the predictions of Aberdeen had come to pass, the war by its very ferocity and completeness forced Britain to wait. It was clear from the totality of the conflict that no balance-of-power situation would result. And then, after the Emancipation Proclamation and Gettysburg the moment for choosing had passed. Only the most pessimistic could doubt that the Union and the continental empire had been saved—saved for democracy, republicanism, and freedom. The Civil War was the capstone and the climax of the era of Manifest Destiny.

I

This book has sought to demonstrate a number of things about young America. It has sought to view American expansionism as an outgrowth of European concepts of empire which, in turn, were inspired here as in Europe by the Romantic Movement. Thus we have viewed political, diplomatic, and militaristic expansionism as an expression of a common culture which spanned the Atlantic and, in a strange way, formulated the rules of a competitive game which Americans and Europeans both understood because of their own common culture. Somehow this lessened the amount of blood shed between the two kindred cultures and made possible the rapprochement so vital in the twentieth century. Although neither culture was willing to concede it at the time, the romantic horizon was big enough for all.

By the same token, this book has also sought to show that "crisis" is never temporary. It is not now and it never was so for the men of the nineteenth century. It goes on, day after day, century after century, even though nations and empires rise and fall, for problems producing crises and demanding solutions are the fundamental lot of man. No such thing as "free security" has ever existed.

This narrative has sought to demonstrate how uncertain and perilous things were by tracing the continual crisis involved in acquiring an empire of any kind. Particularly does the story of young America indicate the degree to which growth and expansion, even at moments of heightened glory, bring with them unforeseen dangers, unwanted commitments, and potentially disastrous responsibilities. Men love power, but they seldom look to the consequences. The history of mid-century American expansionism indicates that the questions of perilous commitment and awesome responsibility that confront the twentieth century were put to mankind a long time ago. The lines of force were set, to the south in the Caribbean, Central America, and South America, and to the west across the wide Pacific to the China Sea. Even our tendency to imitate our European forebears made eventual participation in European conflicts inevitable, despite the advice of the good General Washington.

And so America came to assume its destiny across the romantic world horizon. Full of youthful enthusiasm, it nonetheless learned as it shouldered its way to a prominent place in the world family of nations. The underlying assumption in its long adventure was contained in the dictum of the gentle English romantic poet, William Wordsworth, who once wrote:

The good old rule
Sufficeth them, the simple plan,
That they should take, who have the power,
And they should keep who can.[1]

A philosophy such as this was what made the eagle scream.

---

[1] Quoted in Wallace, *Destiny and Glory*, p. 302.

Suggestions for Additional Reading

The subject of American global and continental expansionism in the first half of the nineteenth century is, of course, a vast one and, as might be expected, it has a corresponding historical literature, rich in color, variety, and human interest. I can do no more here than point out some of the prominent landmarks on the romantic and scholarly horizon of this literature.

GENERAL

There are surprisingly few books which attempt a general interpretation of American expansionism. Of these, by far the best is Richard W. Van Alstyne, *The Rising American Empire* (New York: Oxford University Press, 1960), to which this present book is greatly indebted. Also interesting is the Newberry Library American Studies Symposium, "The Problem of National Destiny," *The Newberry Library Bulletin*, **IV**, 165–191 (August 1957). Another more recent work is Frederick Merk, *Manifest Destiny and Mission in American History* (New York: Alfred A. Knopf, 1963), which attempts by means of a survey of public opinion, largely reflected in newspapers, to make a distinction between those Americans who favored expansion out of a sense of "mission" and those who were expansionists for baser motives. This work addresses itself by implication to the earlier work of Albert K. Weinberg, *Manifest Destiny* (Baltimore: Johns Hopkins Press, 1935), which is a sweeping indictment of all forms of American expansionism. Weinberg, apparently seduced by the "devil theory" of history, purports to see malice and evil intent behind each of the ringing slogans employed to promote expansionism. The usefulness of this book is impaired by the fact that it proves too much, namely, that

Americans everywhere, at all times, and in all situations were grasping and mendacious. It does, however, raise the moral question of expansionism and points up the general aggressiveness of the American character in the last century.

A more specialized work in the same vein is Ramon Ruiz, ed., *The Mexican War—Was It Manifest Destiny?* (New York: Holt, Rinehart and Winston, 1963). This is a book of readings which, despite its apparently narrow focus, raises once again the whole question of Manifest Destiny and its justification. Students may profitably consult also Volumes IV, V, and VI of Samuel Flagg Bemis, ed., *American Secretaries of State and Their Diplomacy* (New York: Alfred A. Knopf, 1928). While these books are valuable insofar as they concern themselves with moral questions, by the same token they tend to polarize inquiry and to prevent a realistic assessment of the power confrontations around the world in this period.

Two further interpretations of American foreign relations and their impact upon the culture are offered by Ralph H. Gabriel in *The Course of American Democratic Thought*, 2nd ed. (New York: Ronald Press, 1956) and in Comer Vann Woodward, "The Age of Reinterpretation," *American Historical Review*, **LXVI**, 1–19, (1960), also issued as *Publication No. 35*, Service Center for Teachers of History, Washington, D. C., 1961. Both of these general works, one by an intellectual historian and the other by a political historian, suggest that mid-nineteenth-century American culture developed in an age of "free security" which meant relative security from external political and economic pressures. The present work demonstrates that this was not so.

THE EXPANSIONISM OF JEFFERSON AND ADAMS

Readers interested in basic source materials should, in addition to the federal documents, consult Hunter Miller, ed., *Treaties and Other International Acts of the United States*, 8 volumes (Washington: Government Printing Office, 1931–1948); Paul Leicester Ford, ed., *The Writings of Thomas Jefferson*, 10 volumes (New York: George Putnam's Sons, 1892–1899); the forthcoming series of *The Papers of Thomas Jefferson*, edited by Julian Boyd; Donald Jackson, ed., *The Letters of the Lewis and Clark Expedition with Related Documents, 1783–1854* (Urbana, Illinois: University of

Illinois Press, 1962); and *The Memoirs of John Quincy Adams Comprising Portions of His Diary from 1795 to 1848*, Charles Francis Adams, ed., 12 volumes (Philadelphia: J. B. Lippincott & Co., 1874–1877). Two more readily available collections of materials on Adams are Allan Nevins, ed., *The Diary of John Quincy Adams*, an abridgement (New York: Charles Scribner's Sons, 1951), and Walter Lafeber, *John Quincy Adams and the American Continental Empire* (Chicago: Quadrangle Books, 1965). Relevant documents may be gleaned from the volumes of W. R. Manning, *Diplomatic Correspondence . . .* , cited below.

The best biographical treatments of the two statesmen are Dumas Malone, *Jefferson and His Time*, 3 volumes (Boston: Little, Brown, and Company, 1948–1962), and Samuel Flagg Bemis, *John Quincy Adams and the Foundations of American Foreign Policy* (New York: Alfred A. Knopf, 1949). The latter, which is the first volume of Bemis' two-volume work on Adams, is a masterpiece, and most relevant to the subject of the present work.

Two classic treatments of the period are Henry Adams, *The History of the United States during the Administrations of Jefferson and Madison*, 9 volumes (New York: Charles Scribner's Sons, 1889–1891), also in an abridged edition, edited by George Dangerfield and Otie Scruggs, 2 volumes (Englewood Cliffs, N. J.: Prentice Hall, Inc., 1963), and George Dangerfield, *The Era of Good Feelings* (New York: Harcourt, Brace, 1952).

Especially useful in dealing with expansion to the south are Arthur Preston Whitaker, *The Spanish-American Frontier, 1783–1795; the Westward Movement and the Spanish Retreat in the Mississippi Valley* (Boston: Houghton Mifflin, 1927), *The Mississippi Question 1795–1803; a Study in Trade, Politics and Diplomacy* (New York and London: Appleton-Century Co., 1934); Thomas P. Abernathy, *The Burr Conspiracy* (New York: Oxford University Press, 1954); Isaac Joslin Cox, *The West Florida Controversy, 1798–1813; A Study in American Diplomacy* (Baltimore: Johns Hopkins Press, 1918), *The Early Exploration of Louisiana* (Cincinnati: University of Cincinnati Press, 1906), "The Louisiana-Texas Frontier," *Quarterly of the Texas State Historical Association*, X, 1–75 (1906); Arthur Preston Whitaker, *The United States and the Independence of Latin America, 1800–1830* (Baltimore: Johns Hopkins Press, 1941); Dexter Perkins, *The Mon-*

roe Doctrine, 1823–1826 (Cambridge, Mass.: Harvard University Press, 1927), *The Monroe Doctrine, 1826–1867* (Baltimore: Johns Hopkins Press, 1933), *A History of the Monroe Doctrine* (Boston: Little, Brown and Co., 1955); J. Fred Rippy, *Rivalry of the United States and Great Britain over Latin America, 1808–1830* (Baltimore: Johns Hopkins Press, 1929); and George W. Kyte, "A Spy on the Western Waters: the Military Intelligence Mission of General Collot in 1796," *Mississippi Valley Historical Review*, **XXXIV**, 427–442 (1947).

Insight into British-American confrontations in the Northwest can be gained from William H. Goetzmann, ed., Washington Irving, *Astoria*, 2 volumes (Philadelphia: J. B. Lippincott, 1961); Frederick Merk, ed., *Fur Trade and Empire* (Cambridge, Mass.: Harvard University Press, 1931), *Albert Gallatin and the Oregon Problem* (Cambridge, Mass.: Harvard University Press, 1950); William Nisbet Chambers, *Old Bullion Benton, Senator from the New West* (Boston: Little, Brown, and Co., 1956); Elbert B. Smith, *Magnificent Missourian: The Life of Thomas Hart Benton* (Philadelphia: J. B. Lippincott and Co., 1958); Henry Nash Smith, *Virgin Land; the American West as Symbol and Myth* (Cambridge, Mass.: Harvard University Press, 1950); Paul C. Phillips, *The Fur Trade*, 2 volumes (Norman, Okla.: University of Oklahoma Press, 1961); Edwin Ernest Rich, *The Hudson's Bay Company, 1670–1870*, 3 volumes (New York: The Macmillan Co., 1961); Richard Oglesby, *Manuel Lisa* (Norman, Okla.: University of Oklahoma Press, 1964); Dale L. Morgan, *Jedediah Smith and the Opening of the West* (Indianapolis: Bobbs-Merrill Co., 1953); and William H. Goetzmann, *Exploration and Empire; the Explorer and the Scientist in the Winning of the American West* (New York: Alfred A. Knopf, 1966). All of these latter books indicate the degree to which a confrontation with Britain in the Northwest was due to the aggressive activities of the fur traders.

THE TEXAN REVOLUTION AND ANNEXATION

For collections of source materials, see Amelia W. Williams and Eugene C. Barker, eds., *The Writings of Sam Houston*, 8 volumes (Austin: University of Texas Press, 1938–1943); Charles A. Gulick and Katherine Elliott, eds., *The Papers of Mirabeau Buonaparte Lamar*, 6 volumes (Austin: A. C. Baldwin and Sons, and

Von Boeckman-Jones, 1921–1928); Eugene C. Barker, "The Austin Papers," *Annual Report of the American Historical Association for the Year 1922*, Vol. II (Washington, D. C., 1928); George P. Garrison, ed., "Diplomatic Correspondence of the Republic of Texas," *Annual Report of the American Historical Association, 1907 and 1908*, 2 volumes (Washington, D. C., 1908, 1911); William C. Binkley, ed., *Official Correspondence of the Texan Revolution, 1835–1836*, 2 volumes (New York: D. Appleton-Century Co., 1956); and William Ray Manning, ed., *Diplomatic Correspondence of the United States: Inter-American Affairs, 1831–1860*, **VIII, IX**, and **XII** (Washington: Carnegie Institute, 1932–1939).

Readable general treatments of various aspects of the Texan Revolution are William C. Binkley, *The Texas Revolution* (Baton Rouge: Louisiana State University Press, 1952); Marquis James, *The Raven, A Biography of Sam Houston* (Indianapolis: Bobbs-Merrill, 1929); Amelia Williams, "A Critical Study of the Siege of the Alamo and the Personnel of Its Defenders," *Southwestern Historical Quarterly* **XXXVI**, 251–287 (1933); Samuel Houston Dixon and Louis Kemp, *The Heroes of San Jacinto* (Houston: Anson Jones Press, 1932); Frank X. Tolbert, *The Day of San Jacinto* (New York: McGraw-Hill, 1959); Lon Tinkle, *Thirteen Days to Glory: The Siege of the Alamo* (New York: McGraw-Hill, 1958); Walter Lord, *A Time to Stand* (New York: Harper and Bros., 1961); Herbert Davenport, "The Men of Goliad," *Southwestern Historical Quarterly*, **XLIII**, 1–41 (1939); Carlos Casteñda, tr., *The Mexican Side of the Texas Revolution* (Dallas: P. L. Turner Co., 1928); and Ralph Wooster, "Texas Military Operations against Mexico, 1842–1843," *Southwestern Historical Quarterly*, **LXVII**, 465–484 (1964).

Other aspects of the Texan Revolution are treated in Samuel H. Lowrie, *Culture Conflict in Texas, 1821–1835* (New York: Columbia University Press, 1932); Gerald Ashford, "Jacksonian Liberalism and Spanish Law in Early Texas," *Southwestern Historical Quarterly*, **LVII**, 1–37 (1953); Eugene C. Barker, "Land Speculation as a Cause of the Texas Revolution," *Quarterly of the Texas State Historical Association*, **X**, 76–95 (1906), "President Jackson and the Texas Revolution," *American Historical Review*, **XII**, 788–809 (1907); Richard R. Stenberg, "The Texas Schemes of Jackson and Houston, 1829–1836," *Southwestern Social Science Quarterly*, **XV**, 229–250 (1934), "Jackson's Neches Claim, 1829–1836,"

Southwestern Historical Quarterly, XXXIX, 255–274 (1936), "President Jackson and Anthony Butler," *Southwest Review*, XXII, 391–404 (1937). The Stenberg articles are of the Weinberg persuasion.

Biographical studies, in addition to *The Raven*, cited above, are Eugene C. Barker, *The Life of Stephen F. Austin* (Nashville and Dallas: Cokesburg Press, 1925); Llerena Friend, *Sam Houston, the Great Designer* (Austin: The University of Texas Press, 1954), an analysis of Houston's later career; Marquis James, *Andrew Jackson*, 2 volumes (Indianapolis: Bobbs-Merrill Co., 1933–1937); Oliver Chitwood, *John Tyler, Champion of the Old South* (New York: Russell and Russell, 1964 reprint ed.); Frank C. Hanighen, *Santa Anna, the Napoleon of the West* (New York: Coward, McCann, 1934); Wilfred H. Callcutt, *Santa Anna: the Story of an Enigma Who Once Was Mexico* (Norman, Okla.: University of Oklahoma Press, 1936); and Herbert P. Gambrell, *Mirabeau Buonaparte Lamar, Troubadour and Crusader* (Dallas: Southwest Press, 1934), *Anson Jones, The Last President of Texas* (New York: Doubleday, 1948). Emmett J. Hughes, *Rebellious Ranger: Rip Ford and the Old Southwest* (Norman, Okla.: University of Oklahoma Press, 1964) is most interesting for its revelation of the difficulties with Mexican guerillas encountered by Scott's army of conquest.

Texan statecraft, expansionism, and the movement toward annexation are treated in Noel Loomis, *The Texan-Santa Fe Pioneers* (Norman, Okla.: University of Oklahoma Press, 1958); Nathaniel W. Stephenson, *Texas and the Mexican War* (New Haven: Yale University Press, 1921); Elgin Williams, *The Animating Pursuit of Speculation; Land Traffic in the Annexation of Texas* (New York: Columbia University Press, 1949); W. C. Binkley, *The Expansionist Movement in Texas 1836–1850* (Berkeley: University of California Press, 1925); Thomas Jefferson Green, *Journal of the Texian Expedition against Mier . . .* repr. (Austin: The Steck Co., 1935); Joseph W. Schmitz, *Texan Statecraft 1836–1845* (San Antonio: The Naylor Co., 1941); Kinley Brauer, "Massachusetts State Texas Committee—Last Stand against the Annexation of Texas," *Journal of American History*, LI, 214–231 (1964); Richard Stenberg, "President Polk and the Annexation of Texas," *Southwestern Social Science Quarterly*, XIV, 333–356 (1934); Pierre Laurent, "Belgium's Relations with Texas and the United States,

1839–44," *Southwestern Historical Quarterly*, **LXVIII**, 220–236 (1964); Harriet Smither, "English Abolitionism and the Annexation of Texas," *Southwestern Historical Quarterly*, **XXXII**, 193–205 (1929); R. A. McLemore, "The Influence of French Diplomatic Policy on the Annexation of Texas," *Southwestern Historical Quarterly*, **XLIII**, 342–347 (1940); and Joseph Milton Nance, *After San Jacinto; The Texas-Mexican Frontier, 1836–1841* (Austin: University of Texas Press, 1963), *Attack and Counterattack; The Texas-Mexican Frontier, 1842* (Austin: University of Texas Press, 1964).

Major works relating the general framework of United States, Texan, and Mexican relations are Ephraim D. Adams, *British Interests and Activities in Texas 1838–1846* (Baltimore: Johns Hopkins Press, 1910), a very influential work that has more often than not been carelessly read by historians; Eugene C. Barker, *Mexico and Texas 1821–1835* (Dallas: P. L. Turner Co., 1928); William R. Manning, *Early Diplomatic Relations between the United States and Mexico* (Baltimore: Johns Hopkins Press, 1916); J. Fred Rippy, *The United States and Mexico* (New York: Alfred A. Knopf, 1926); James M. Callahan, *American Foreign Policy in Mexican Relations* (New York: The Macmillan Co., 1922); Justin H. Smith, *The Annexation of Texas* (New York: Baker and Taylor Co., 1911), a prelude to his later work on the Mexican War, but the standard work on the subject; and George L. Rives, *The United States and Mexico, 1821–1848*, 2 volumes (New York: Charles Scribner's Sons, 1913), the most detailed and comprehensive treatment of the whole period, an indispensable work.

OREGON AND CALIFORNIA

The most important recent interpretation of American expansionist policy with regard to Oregon and California is Norman Graebner, *Empire on the Pacific, A Study in American Continental Expansion* (New York: Ronald Press, 1955).

Part of the difficulty in assessing the motives for expansion stems from the enigmatic character of the source materials. William Ray Manning's *Diplomatic Correspondence of the United States: Canadian Relations, 1784–1860*, 4 volumes (Washington: Carnegie Institute, 1940–1945), presents the official correspondence relating to Oregon; John Bassett Moore, *The Works of James*

Buchanan, 12 volumes (Philadelphia: J. B. Lippincott, 1908–1911) presents Buchanan's thoughts but not Polk's; the monumental *The Larkin Papers*, 10 volumes (Berkeley: University of California Press, 1951–1964), edited by George P. Hammond, presents Larkin's opinions and instructions, but only one side of a complex situation. Captain Charles Wilkes, *Narrative of the United States Exploring Expedition. During the Years 1838, 1839, 1840, 1841, 1842*, 5 volumes (Philadelphia: Lea and Blanchard, 1845) only serves to confuse the issue, and Milo Milton Quaife, ed., *The Diary of James K. Polk During His Presidency, 1845 to 1849*, 4 volumes (Chicago: A. C. McClurg and Co., 1910) leaves the reader with the enigma that was President James K. Polk—a simple man on paper. For an abridged version of Polk's diary, see Allan Nevins, ed., *Polk, The Diary of a President, 1845 to 1849* (London, New York, and Toronto: Longmans, Green and Co., 1929). This contains an excellent short sketch of Polk's life and some shrewd speculation as to his personality.

Two interesting biographies are Eugene McCormac, *James K. Polk: A Political Biography* (Berkeley: University of California Press, 1922), which concentrates on Polk's public career, and Charles Greer Sellers, *James K. Polk, Jacksonian, 1795–1843* (Princeton, N. J.: Princeton University Press, 1957), which humanizes Polk but unfortunately in this volume does not reach the presidential period.

Bernard De Voto in *The Year of Decision* (Boston: Houghton Mifflin, 1943) manages to suggest something of the complexity of motives behind the movement to the Pacific which had bearing on official policy. Jesse S. Reeves, *American Diplomacy under Tyler and Polk* (Baltimore: Johns Hopkins Press, 1907) is a standard work, but outdated. John C. Ewers, ed., *The Adventures of Zenas Leonard, Fur Trader* (Norman, Okla.: University of Oklahoma Press, 1959) is a good example of the early American vision of the Pacific Coast. Robert G. Albion, *The Rise of New York Port, 1815–1860* (New York: Charles Scribner's Sons, 1939), and Clement Eaton, *The Growth of Southern Civilization 1790–1860* (New York: Harper and Bros., 1961) give clues as to the interrelation of the southern planter, the northeastern shipper, and the English bankers and manufacturers. The reader interested in this subject should consult the histories of various British and American banking firms, particularly those of Brown Brothers and the house of

Baring. John S. Galbraith, *The Hudson's Bay Company as an Imperial Factor, 1821–1869* (Berkeley: University of California Press, 1957) details the relationship between British economic and political interests in the Northwest. Further material on British policy throughout the period is to be found in Charles K. Webster, *The Foreign Policy of Castlereagh, 1815–1822* (London: G. Bell and Sons, 1925), and *The Foreign Policy of Palmerston 1830–1841* (London: G. Bell and Sons, 1951); Harold Temperly, *The Foreign Policy of Canning, 1822–1827* (London: G. Bell and Sons, 1928); and Bradford Perkins, *Castlereagh and Adams; England and the United States, 1812–1823* (Berkeley: University of California Press, 1964). A. P. Nasatir, *French Activities in California, an Archival Calendar Guide* (Palo Alto, Calif.: Stanford University Press, 1945) presents an indication of French interest in California.

A minor tempest rages about the question of Frémont's mission to California in 1845. Allan Nevins in *Frémont, Pathmaker of the West* (New York, London: D. Appleton-Century Co., 1939) believes Frémont had orders from Polk to subvert California, as does Richard Stenberg in "Polk and Frémont, 1845–1846," *Pacific Historical Review*, **VII**, 211–227 (1938). George Tays in "Frémont Had No Secret Instructions," *Pacific Historical Review*, **IX**, 151–171 (1940), and John A. Hussey, "The Origin of the Gillespie Mission," *California Historical Society Quarterly*, **XIX**, 43–58 (1940) do not.

Some of the more important articles bearing on the Oregon-California question are Frederick Merk, "British Government Propaganda and the Oregon Treaty," *American Historical Review*, **XL**, 38–62 (1934), "The British Corn Crisis of 1845–1846 and the Oregon Treaty," *Agricultural History*, **VIII**, 95–123 (1935), "The Oregon Pioneers and the Boundary," *American Historical Review*, **XXIX**, 681–699 (1924), "British Party Politics and the Oregon Treaty," *American Historical Review*, **XXXVII**, 653–677 (1932); Norman A. Graebner, "Maritime Factors in the Oregon Compromise," *Pacific Historical Review*, **XX**, 331–345 (1951), "American Interest in California, 1845," *Pacific Historical Review*, **XXII**, 12–28 (1953); Robert Glass Cleland, "Early Sentiment for the Annexation of California; an Account of the Growth of American Interest in California, 1835–1846," *Southwestern Historical Quarterly*, **XVIII**, 1–40 (1914); Wilbur D. Jones and J. Chal Vinson, "British Preparedness and the Oregon Settlement," *Pacific*

Historical Review, **XXII**, 353–364 (1953); Richard W. Van Alstyne, "International Rivalries in the Pacific Northwest," *Oregon Historical Quarterly*, **XLVI**, 185–218 (1945).

Two other articles are of interest: Edwin A. Miles, "Fifty-Four Forty or Fight—An American Political Legend," *Mississippi Valley Historical Review*, **XLIV**, 291–309 (1957), and Julius W. Pratt, "The Origin of Manifest Destiny," *American Historical Review*, **XXXII**, 795–798 (1927).

THE MEXICAN WAR

The Mexican War is America's "forgotten war." There exists no extended modern study of this important conflict. This is perhaps because the standard work on the subject, Justin H. Smith, *The War with Mexico*, 2 volumes (New York: The Macmillan Co., 1919) is so massively researched that it is difficult to add more to the story beyond new interpretation, which is badly needed. Other treatments of the Mexican War are for various reasons less satisfactory than Smith's. They are Alfred Hoyt Bill, *Rehearsal for Conflict* (New York: Alfred A. Knopf, 1947), which treats the war as simply a prelude to the Civil War; Robert Selph Henry, *The Story of the Mexican War* (Indianapolis: Bobbs-Merrill, 1950), the best brief treatment of the war; and Otis A. Singletary, *The Mexican War* (Chicago: University of Chicago Press, 1960), most readily available in paperback. William H. Goetzmann, *Army Exploration in the American West 1803–1863* (New Haven: Yale University Press, 1959) provides information concerning the effect of the war on public policy and the development of American geographical knowledge about the Far West. Henry Haferkorn, *The War with Mexico, 1846–1848: A Select Bibliography on the Causes, Conduct, and Political Aspects of the War* (Washington: U. S. Engineer School, 1944) is a useful bibliography with occasional annotations.

Biographies and studies of the leading figures in the war are abundant. Some of the best are James P. Shenton, *Robert John Walker, A Politician from Jackson to Lincoln* (New York: Columbia University Press, 1961); Charles Winslow Elliott, *Winfield Scott, the Soldier and the Man* (New York: The Macmillan Co., 1937); Hudson Strode, *Jefferson Davis, American Patriot* (New York: Harcourt, Brace, 1955); Lloyd Lewis, *Captain Sam Grant* (Boston: Little, Brown and Co., 1950); Holman Hamilton, *Zachary*

Taylor, 2 volumes (Indianapolis: Bobbs-Merrill Co., 1941–1951); and Edward S. Wallace, *General William Jenkins Worth, Monterrey's Forgotten Hero* (Dallas: Southern Methodist University Press, 1953). The interested student should by all means consult the wealth of contemporary diaries and memoirs of the Mexican War participants, since they form the richest and most rewarding literature on the period. The best of these is Samuel E. Chamberlain, *My Confession* (New York: Harper and Bros., 1956). Also see Albert C. Ramsey, ed., *The Other Side: Or, Notes for the History of the War between Mexico and the United States* (New York: Wiley, 1850).

Background materials for the war can be found in H. H. Bancroft, *The History of Mexico*, Vol. V (San Francisco: A. L. Bancroft, 1887), *The History of the North Mexican States and Texas*, Vol. II (San Francisco: A. L. Bancroft, 1889); Stella Drumm, ed., *Down the Santa Fe Trail and into Mexico* (New Haven: Yale University Press, 1926); and Paul Horgan, *Great River: The Rio Grande in North American History*, 2 volumes (New York: Rinehart and Co., 1954).

Specialized subjects are treated in the following: J. D. P. Fuller, *The Movement for the Acquisition of All Mexico, 1846–1848* (Baltimore: Johns Hopkins Press, 1936); John T. Hughes, *Doniphan's Expedition* (Cincinnati: U. P. James, 1847, reprinted, Washington: Government Printing Office, 1914); Robert A. Brent, "Nicholas P. Trist and the Treaty of Guadalupe Hidalgo," *Southwestern Historical Quarterly*, LVII, 454–474 (1945); U. S. Library of Congress, Division of Maps, [Laurence Martin], *Disturnell's Map* (Washington: Govt. Printing Office, 1937); Richard Stenberg, "The Failure of Polk's Mexican War Intrigue of 1845," *Pacific Historical Review*, IV, 39–68 (1935); M. S. Beach, "Communication: A Secret Mission to Mexico," *Scribner's Monthly*, XVIII, 136–140 (May, 1879); Louis Sears, "Nicholas P. Trist, a Diplomat with Ideals," *Mississippi Valley Historical Review*, XI, 85–98 (1924). The latter is the only significant study of a much-neglected but fascinating person.

CARIBBEAN AND ISTHMIAN DIPLOMACY

On relations concerning Cuba, see Basil Rauch, *American Interest in Cuba: 1848-1855* (New York: Columbia University Press, 1948); Amos A. Ettinger, *The Mission to Spain of Pierre*

Soulé, 1853-55 (New Haven: Yale University Press, 1932); W. A. Swanberg, *Sickles the Incredible* (New York: Charles Scribner's Sons, 1956); Anderson C. Quisenbery, *Lopez's Expeditions to Cuba, 1850 and 1851* (Louisville, Ky.: J. P. Morton and Co., 1906); R. C. Caldwell, *The Lopez Expedition to Cuba, 1848-1851* (Princeton, N. J.: Princeton University Press, 1915); and J. Preston Moore, "Pierre Soulé: Southern Expansionist and Promoter," *The Journal of Southern History*, XXI 203-223 (1955).

For general background on the history of Central America, see H. H. Bancroft, *Central America*, 3 volumes (San Francisco: A. L. Bancroft, 1882-1887). Also, see John Lloyd Stephens, *Incidents of Travel in Central America, Chiapas, and Yucatan*, new edition, 2 volumes in one (Rutgers, New Jersey: Rutgers University Press, 1949), or Victor W. von Hagen's 2-volume ed., *Incidents of Travel in Yucatan* (Norman, Okla.: University of Oklahoma Press, 1962); Ephraim George Squier, *Nicaragua; Its People, Scenery, Monuments, Resources, Condition, and Proposed Canal* (New York: Harper and Bros., 1860), and *The Serpent Symbol and the Worship of the Reciprocal Principle of Nature in America* (New York: George Putnam's Sons, 1851). For source material, William R. Manning, ed., *Diplomatic Correspondence of the United States: Inter-American Affairs, 1831–1860*, III, IV, VI, VII, XI (Washington: Carnegie Institute, 1932–1939) is indispensable.

The most complete and enjoyable book on the filibusters is Edward S. Wallace, *Destiny and Glory* (New York: Coward-McCann, 1957), but also see William Oscar Scruggs, *Filibusters and Financiers; The Story of William Walker and His Associates* (New York: The Macmillan Co., 1916); Mary A. Williamson, "The Secessionist Diplomacy of Yucatan," *Hispanic-American Historical Review;*, IX, 132-143 (1929); Roy F. Nichols, *Franklin Pierce, Young Hickory of the Granite Hills* (Philadelphia: University of Pennsylvania Press, 1958); Richard W. Van Alstyne, "American Filibustering and the British Navy: A Caribbean Analogue of Mediterranean 'Piracy,'" *American Journal of the Institute of Law*, XXXII, 138-142 (1938); and William Walker, *The War in Nicaragua* (Mobile, New York: S. H. Goetzel, 1860). A recent reinterpretation of Walker's role is Albert Carr, *The World and William Walker* (New York: Harper and Row, 1963).

More specialized works relating to Caribbean and Isthmian

matters, as well as transportation routes to the Pacific, are Paul Neff Garber, *The Gadsden Treaty* (Philadelphia: University of Pennsylvania Press, 1923); William H. Goetzmann, "The Mexican Boundary Survey, 1848-1853," *Southwestern Historical Quarterly;*, **LXII**, 141-163 (1958); Robert Russel, *Improvement of Communication with the Pacific Coast as an Issue in American Politics, 1783-1864,* (Cedar Rapids, Iowa: The Torch Press, 1948); and Richard W. Van Alstyne, "The Central American Policies of Lord Palmerston, 1846-1848," *Hispanic American Historical Review,* **XVI**, 341-359 (1936), "British Diplomacy and the Clayton-Bulwer Treaty, 1850-1860," *Journal of Modern History,* **XI**, 149-183 (1939), "British Statesmen on the Clayton-Bulwer Treaty and American Expansion," *American Historical Review;*, **XLII**, 491-500 (1936-1937).

THE PACIFIC AND THE FAR EAST

The most fascinating background for assessing the reasons for American and European interest in the Pacific and Far East is provided by Bernard Smith's important *The European Vision and the South Pacific 1768-1850* (Oxford: Oxford University Press, 1960). Besides his own narrative, see the rather thin biography of Captain Charles Wilkes by Daniel Henderson, *The Hidden Coasts* (New York: William Sloan Associates, 1953). In decided contrast to this is Samuel Eliot Morison's classic, *The Maritime History of Massachusetts* (Boston and New York: Houghton Mifflin, 1921). Also of interest is R. F. Almy, "J. N. Reynolds; A Brief Biography with Reference to Poe and Symmes," *The Colophon,* **II**, 227-245 (1937). In addition, see J. N. Reynolds, *Voyage of the United States Frigate Potomac . . . During the Circumnavigation of the Globe in the Years 1831, 1832, 1833 and 1834* (New York: Harper and Bros., 1835), *Address on the Subject of a Surveying and Exploring Expedition to the Pacific Ocean and South Seas . . .* (New York: Harper and Bros., 1836).

On Americans in East Asia see Tyler Dennett, *Americans in Eastern Asia* (New York: The Macmillan Co., 1922); Earl Swisher, *China's Management of the American Barbarians: A Study of Sino-American Relations, 1841-1861, with Documents* (New Haven: Yale University Press, 1953); Arthur Cole, ed, *Yankee Surveyors in the Shogun's Seas* (Princeton, N. J.: Princeton University

Press, 1947); Carl Crow, *He Opened the Door of Japan; Townsend Harris and the Story of His Amazing Adventures in Establishing American Relations with the Far East* (New York and London: Harper and Brothers, 1939); John K. Fairbank, *Trade and Diplomacy on the China Coast, the Opening of the Treaty Ports, 1842-1854*, 2 volumes (Cambridge, Mass.: Harvard University Press, 1953); Henry F. Graff, *Bluejackets with Perry in Japan* . . . (New York: New York Public Library, 1952); Arthur C. Walworth, *Black Ships off Japan: the Story of Commodore Perry's Expedition* (New York: Alfred A. Knopf, Inc., 1946); and the general work, Foster Rhea Dulles, *America in the Pacific* (Boston: Houghton Mifflin, 1938) which also touches on Hawaii. Dulles' new book, *Yankees and Samurai; America's Role in the Emergence of Modern Japan: 1791-1900* (New York: Harper and Row, 1965) arrived as this book was going to press.

Further materials on Hawaii can be gleaned from Harold Whitman Bradley, *The American Frontier in Hawaii, The Pioneers 1789-1843* (Palo Alto, Calif.: Stanford University Press, 1942); Sylvester K. Stevens, *American Expansionism in Hawaii 1842-1898* (Harrisburg, Pa.: Archives Publishing Co., 1945); and Ralph S. Kuykendall, *The Hawaiian Kingdom, 1778–1854, Foundation and Transformation* (Honolulu: University of Hawaii [Press], 1938).

Index

Aberdeen, Lord, diplomacy of, 34, 47, 51; foresees American Civil War, 51, 104

Abert, J. J., 59

Abolitionism, 33-34, 36, 51-52, see also Civil War; Slavery

Adams, Ephraim D., 23, 51

Adams, John Quincy, and expansionism, 1-3, 11, 15, 18-19, 22, 38; background of, 2; as Secretary of State, 2, 11, 16-19; politics of, 2; and securing of Northwest, 11-13, 16, 44; and Florida, 13-15; and Monroe Doctrine, 16-19; and Latin American independence, 18; and freedom of the seas, 18; as President, 20; desire of, to acquire Texas, 21, 24, 26; and abolitionism, 33, 51; diary of, 39; interest of, in exploration, 96

Adventurers, see Filibusters

Age of Discovery, 92

Agrarian interests, see Farmers

Alamo, battle of, 30, 31, 32

Alaska, proposed expansion into, 91, 93, 103

Aleman, Luis, 27

Alexander, Prince (Hawaiian), 103

Almonte, Juan N., on annexation of Texas, 40, 55, 59; and peace negotiations, 69

America, Central, see Latin America

American Intervention, War of the, see Mexican War

Americans, character of, xiv; use of Mississippi by, 6-7; and world opinion, 75

Amiens, Peace of, see Peace of Amiens

Amoy, 96

Ampudia, Pedro, 63

Anahuac, Texas, customs house at, 27; garrison at, 29

Anglo-Chinese War, see Opium War

Annexation, Hawaiian, 103

Antarctica, U.S. claims to, xiv, xv, 96

Anti-Americanism, of Santa Anna, 57

Arbuthnot, Alexander, 13

Arista, Mariano, 60, 61

Arizona, 21, 72

Arkansas River, in Louisiana Purchase, 14; and Texas boundary, 15, 16

Armbrister, Robert, 13

Armijo, Manuel, 66

Armstrong, James, 101

Armstrong, Richard, 102

Army, Mexican, in Texas, 27, 31-32; and Mexican War, 61

 Texan, creation of, 29; U.S. volunteers in, 29, 30, 32; quarrels within, 29-30; financing of, 32

 United States, during Mexican War, 54, 58, 62, 66-67

Army of the West, 62, 66-67

Articles of Confederation, 94

on, 9, 41-43; international rivalry on, 19, 42, 43; Texas plan to expand to, 33; U.S. seeks ports on, 39, 44, 48, 49, 50, 56; U.S. boundaries to, 56, 60, 72; communications routes to, 74; railroad to, 89; exploration of, 96; *see also* Oregon; Northwest, the

Pacific Mail Steamship Company, 83

Pacific Ocean, 6; U.S. activities on, xiv, 9, 73, 91, 95; confrontations across, xiv, 105; British exploration of, 3, 96; Canadian Northwest Company expands to, 4; trade across, 9, 94; diplomacy about, 24; history of, 40-46; Central American crossings to, 84, 85; dangers of trade on, 94-95; coaling stations on, 99

Pacific Squadron, *see* United States Pacific Squadron

Pago Pago, Samoa, 96

Paine, Tom, 1

Pakenham, Richard, debate of, with Calhoun, 36, 52; and Northwest boundary, 47

Palmer, Nathaniel, 96

Palo Alto, battle of, 61, 63

Panama, commerce in, 83 Isthmus of, transit across, 75-76; railway across, 83-84

Panama Canal, forerunners of, 76

Panama Railway Company, 83, 88

Panton-Leslie Company, 13

Paredes, Mariano, 55-56, 57, 60

Paris, 3, 7-9, 85

Parker, Dr. Peter, 100-101

Parrott, William S., 59-60

Patagonia, 3

Paulet, George, 103

Peace of Amiens, 8

Peace party, Mexican, 68, 70; Texan, 27-28

Pecos River, and Texas boundary, 21

Peel, Sir Robert, 47

Peking, China, Europeans in, 101

Peña y Peña, Manuel, 59-60

Pensacola, Florida, 13, 60

Perry, Matthew C., 98-99

Peru, 56

Philippines, 95, 98, 100

Philosophies, Eastern, 92-93

Philosophy, and expansionism, 93

Pierce, Franklin, 71, 103

Pike, Zebulon, 14

Pinckney, Charles C., 7

Pinto, Juan Mendez, 92

Pirates, off Malaya, 92; off Java, 94

Plains of Mesa, battle of, 67

Poe, Edgar Allan, 81

Poinsett, Joel, 21-22

Polk, James K., political career of, 36-37, 38, 43, 49, 50; and Texas annexation, 36-37; compared to Jackson, 38; expansionism of, 38, 46-47, 49; nature of, 38-39, 48, 58; objectives of, 39; historians on, 39; diary of, 39, 46; Oregon policy of, 43, 46-48, 49, 50; free trade policy of, 47, 50 n.; diplomacy of, 48-49, 50, 73; and shipping interests, 49; and Mexican War, 57, 58-60, 61, 62, 63, 69, 71, 72-73; death of, 73, 80; interest of, in Caribbean, 75, 76-77; interest of, in Central America, 76, 80

Porter, David, 95

Potomac, in Pacific, 95

Price, Sterling, 67

Priestly, Joseph, 1

Princeton, 36

Privateers, opposition to, 18

Public opinion, United States, Texan appeal to, 35-36; support of Walker by, 86

Puget Sound, 43, 49; and Polk, 39, 46; importance of, 44, 50; exploration of, 44, 96; as boundary for U.S., 45

Puget Sound Agricultural Company, 47

Quitman, General John A., 78

DATE DUE

OCT 1 9 1994			
APR 1 9 1995			